'This book is written by someone who knows o̶ and turmoil of those adapting to the knowledge̶ He also knows how people fluctuate in their̶ approaching and yet wish to live. Cicely Saunders said that "dignity is having a sense of personal worth". Connecting with people is fundamental to restoring the sense of a person's worth, understanding them in the unique biographical context of their life. Some turn to religious faith, some turn away. But all need to know their uniqueness is respected and need to be listened to. Hope then emerges again; realistic hope for what can be achieved and acceptance of what cannot, hope to complete life's tasks well, hope to do whatever the individual needs in the time left. And hope is confirmed in the secure knowledge that they will not be abandoned. The author's experience of "being there", advocating for patients and giving voice to those who feel they are becoming voiceless underpin his writings. His remit concerns spirituality and personhood far more than any particular religious faith. His work is truly uplifting as it restores the essence of being.'

— *Baroness Ilora Finlay, Professor of Palliative Medicine and Independent Crossbench member of the House of Lords*

'Steve Nolan clears away the clutter and gets to the very heart of spiritual care. He explores the human capacity to "stare into the sun" of one's own mortality, and invites an authentic engagement with the dying, which offers hope beyond recovery. This book, which is all about "being-with" the other, in the depths, shifts perceptions of ̶opeful journeying and spiritual care and is an essential read for all ̶ho care for the dying soul.'

— *Ian Stirling, Editor, Scottish Journal of Healthcare Chaplaincy and Association of Hospice and Palliative Care Chaplains*

̶essible, engaging and informative a compelling read, striking at ̶eart of what is important to those who are dying. Complex and ̶ive issues explored with honesty, sensitivity and integrity. This ̶ has the potential to transform how matters of death, dying and ̶ality are addressed by all those providing end of life care.'

̶ilf McSherry, Professor of Dignity in Care for Older People, Staffordshire University and The Shrewsbury and Telford Hospital NHS Trust

'This is an extraordinary book. Steve Nolan invites his readers to enter into those intimate moments between the health care professional and the person who is dying in which hopes and fears are held together in sometimes painful but beautiful experiences of spiritual integrity. The book draws on material from interviews with hospice chaplains, but its insights into spiritual care have much to offer any worker in palliative care services. Using the concept of "dwelling", Nolan explores the idea of the worker as "presence" – a dynamic interaction between two people in proximity to death in which my death and death of another become fused. We often talk about empathy in this field, but Steve Nolan has explored empathy with the person who is dying in all its demanding, challenging and privileging richness.'

— *Margaret Holloway, Professor of Social Work and Director of the Centre for Spirituality Studies, University of Hull*

Spiritual Care at the End of Life

The Chaplain as a 'Hopeful Presence'

Steve Nolan

Foreword by Dr Rowan Williams

Jessica Kingsley *Publishers*
London and Philadelphia

Cover image generously supplied by Annie Soudain www.anniesoudain.co.uk

First published in 2012
by Jessica Kingsley Publishers
116 Pentonville Road
London N1 9JB, UK
and
400 Market Street, Suite 400
Philadelphia, PA 19106, USA

www.jkp.com

Library of Congress Cataloging in Publication Data
Nolan, Steve.
  Spiritual care at the end of life : the chaplain as a "hopeful presence" / Steve Nolan.
    p. cm.
  Includes bibliographical references and index.
  ISBN 978-1-84905-199-6 (alk. paper)
  1. Church work with the terminally ill. 2. Terminally ill--Religious
life. I. Title. II. Title: Chaplain as a "hopeful presence".
  BV4338.N65 2012
  259'.4175--dc23
                                        2011021195

British Library Cataloguing in Publication Data
A CIP catalogue record for this book is available from the British Library

ISBN 978 1 84905 199 6
eISBN 978 0 85700 513 7

Printed and bound in Great Britain

For the people who have touched my life —
some I will always remember,
some I can never forget;
and some have changed me.

Contents

Foreword

Britain has led the world in developing a fully professional approach to palliative care and end-of-life challenges; speaking to those in other countries who are eager to move in similar directions gives one a very vivid sense of how far we have come. But at a time when the entire world of healthcare in the UK is changing fast, there is no room for complacency. And one of the most valuable things about Steve Nolan's book is that it offers insights and perspectives that are relevant for all healthcare professionals, not only those responsible for spiritual care in the last days of a person's life.

Indeed, the way in which he helps us arrive at a clear definition of spiritual care is itself a valuable contribution in a climate where there is, as he notes, a certain amount of scepticism about the funding of chaplaincy from public funds. In essence, what he is concerned with is how a person facing the end of their life is helped to 'own' that process and that moment in appropriate ways, how they can come to see themselves as having both dignity and freedom in these circumstances. He takes us through a very careful and perceptive discussion of what hope does and doesn't mean for a dying person, focusing on notions of 'absolute' or 'ultimate' hope that are not about specific desired outcomes but about the refusal to identify oneself with an inevitable future and the consequent liberty to engage with each moment and each meeting as they emerge.

This kind of hope, Nolan argues, is what is nourished by the 'hopeful presence' of the chaplain – someone who is willing simply to be with the dying person without any prescribed outcomes limiting the relationship. This means acceptance by the chaplain that they will first be an 'evocative' presence (triggering negative as well as positive projection) and then, assuming a relatively positive response, an 'accompanying' and a 'comforting' presence (comforting in the sense of strengthening, not just consoling).

Out of this comes the 'hopeful' presence which releases in the dying person that liberty to be more than passive in the face of death.

But this process has implications for the chaplain too – and for other carers. Inevitably it evokes the mortality of the carer; and Nolan stresses that this entails a willingness on the part of the carer to be changed by the encounter. This does not mean a sacrifice of proper professional detachment; but it does mean knowing how to distinguish this from plain denial. Boundaries are there precisely because this is difficult territory where we are always to some extent at risk. He raises the very important issue of how far our current philosophies and practices of nursing training equip nurses for this. He warns – rightly, I believe – of the dangers of loading expectations on to the nursing profession without thinking through how people are given not just the education but – as a religious teacher might put it – the personal *formation* to cope with their situation without taking refuge in an evasive pseudo-professionalism that defends them in the wrong ways from the risks of encounter.

All this is framed in the context of a well-constructed research project and illustrated with personal material from a range of practitioners – including some moving narrative from the author himself. The whole book describes a model of spiritual care that is about the needs of professionals as well as patients and sketches a genuinely transformative vision of what it might look like. Managers and fundholders in NHS trusts would do well to think about the questions so intelligently discussed here – and the stories told – before assuming that spiritual care is no more than a private affair for the religiously-minded minority. 'Presence' is something impossible to quantify as to its results, especially in the context of end-of-life care; but its human significance (for the giver and the receiver of care) *can* be mapped and explored, and Steve Nolan has done a fine job of opening up this crucial area in fresh and challenging ways.

Dr Rowan Williams
Archbishop of Canterbury
Lambeth Palace
November 2011

Acknowledgements

I am grateful to Cheryl Hunt (*Journal for the Study of Spirituality*) and Eric Stoddart (*Practical Theology*) of Equinox Publishing, Colette Reid (*Palliative Medicine*) of SAGE, Derek Sellman (*Nursing Philosophy*) of Wiley-Blackwell, and Max Watson, Caroline Lucas, Andrew Hoy and Jo Wells (*The Oxford Handbook of Palliative Care*) of Oxford University Press for permission to use material that has previously appeared in their publications.

Introduction

One's mere presence will mean much; one's sensitive responsiveness to the feelings of the dying will mean even more.

Norman Autton (1968). *Pastoral Care in Hospitals.*
London: SPCK, p.46

As a punishment on men, following Prometheus' theft of fire from the gods, Zeus created a woman. Bestowed with all the gifts of the gods, Pandora must have seemed a very curious kind of punishment; but like Eve, her weak-willed sister in myth, Pandora was destined to be the earth mother of all suffering. Opening her infamous box, she set loose the evils and pains that have since beset all human experience, and when she did manage to close the lid, only one item remained ... hope.

Modern healthcare professionals attach great importance to enabling dying people to maintain hope in the teeth of suffering and many healthcarers who write about hope take the view that it has therapeutic value. According to Nekolaichuk and Bruera (1998), 'Hope plays an important role in effective coping, enhances quality of life, and may influence the immune system' (p.36). Chi (2007) says that, 'Hope is considered an effective coping strategy for patients with cancer, providing adaptive power to help them get through the difficult situation and achieve desired goals' (p.415).

Pandora may have kept hope safe to benefit those who are suffering, but the therapeutic value of what she managed to salvage presents modern palliative healthcarers with a very real dilemma. Garrard and Wrigley (2009) succinctly describe the ethical problem:

In order to maintain hope in a terminally-ill patient, the kind of hope that would prevent a descent into depression and despair, it seems that the health-care

> practitioner might have to deceive the patient in some
> way about the likely (in some cases well-nigh certain)
> outcome of her illness. (Garrard and Wrigley 2009, p.38)

As they explain, healthcarers who do 'deceive' a person for whom
they are caring may act from benevolent intentions; but that is a
poor defence against disrespecting or disregarding their autonomy.

This kind of healthcare dilemma brings the stuff of ethics right
down to ward level. However, while I am conscious in this book
that this kind of dilemma is an everyday fact of healthcare decision-
making, my focus will be more existential: I am concerned with
those people who know they are facing death, and who know there
is no hope of recovery. In particular, I am concerned with how
chaplains care for people who are navigating the precarious route
between hope (Latin: *sperare* 'to hope') and despair (Latin: *desperare*
'despair' [*de* 'off, from']).

According to Yalom (1980), 'the physicality of death destroys
man, [but] the idea of death saves him' (p.30). By this he means
(following Heidegger) that 'the tranquillized everydayness'
(Heidegger 1962, p.297), in which one inauthentically covers up the
certainty of one's own death, yields to the anticipation that death is
one's '*ownmost possibility – non-relational, certain and as such indefinite,
not to be outstripped*' (p.303). Yalom's point is that life experiences,
such as grief, major decisions or anniversaries, relationship break-
ups, or the diagnosis of a life-threatening illness can be what he
calls an 'awakening experience' (2008, pp.31–75). Such events are
a kind of 'jolting, irreversible experience which shifts the individual
from the everyday mode to a more authentic mode [of which] death
is by far the most potent' (Yalom 2000). As a consequence, news
that they have cancer or some other life-threatening illness may
shift a person from everyday '*forgetfulness of being*' to the 'state of
mindfulness of being' (Yalom 1980, pp.30–1).

If Yalom is right, perhaps healthcarers would do well to
encourage people to confront their anxieties about dying, face
their despair and so somehow 'awaken'. However, despite Yalom's
observation that 'cancer cures psychoneurosis and death bestows
an unmistakable bitter-sweet poignancy to life' (2000), others are
less sanguine. Nekolaichuk and Bruera (1998) urge 'respect for the

value of hope in oncology and palliative care' (p.39), while Kübler-Ross (1969) rejects doing anything that might dismantle hope and maintains that hope is psychologically nourishing and that a person who is dying needs to maintain hope. Indeed, existential psychotherapists Cooper and Adams (2005), warn that there is 'little direct evidence that individuals who acknowledge their beingness-towards-death, in all its existential anxiety, experience lower levels of neurotic anxiety' (pp.84–85); and as Yalom (1980) concedes, this may be because death anxiety 'exists at the deepest levels of being, is heavily repressed, and is rarely experienced in its full sense' (p.188).

One reason why authentic anticipation of one's death, one's *ownmost possibility*, may increase neurotic anxiety and precipitate a fall into despair (Cooper and Adams 2005, p.85) could be, as Camus (2005) suggests, that it poses the absurdity of life and with it the 'one truly serious philosophical problem' (p.1), namely suicide as 'a solution to the absurd' (p.5). Echoing Heidegger, Camus finds a form of heroic hope in consciously accepting the 'absurdity and indifference of the universe, and [affirming] all the more strongly the values and pleasures of humanity itself' (Matthews 1996, p.84), and, together with Sophocles' hero, concluding 'all is well' (Camus 2005, p.118). However, Camus' existential heroism runs counter to the heroism of existential psychotherapist Frankl (2004) for whom finding meaning is the avenue by which 'even the helpless victim of a hopeless situation, facing a fate he cannot change, may rise above himself' (p.147) and so find hope. For Frankl, the opportunity to be proud of one's suffering is ennobling, and he links hope with 'the defiant power of the human spirit' (p.147).

It may follow from this that lack of hope (*desperare*) is diagnostic of dis-ease within the human spirit, the cause of which is a lack of meaning. Certainly, within the nursing/medical literature, Frankl's philosophical perspective finds resonance in Saunders (1988), who connects spiritual pain with lack of meaning. As Rumbold (1986) observes, the equation of suffering with spiritual distress, and the corollary that spiritual distress is pathological, seems intrinsic within nursing/medical literature:

> in medical usage [hope] seems to be limited implicitly to hope for recovery or survival…. The object of hope in most clinical literature is a future in which the patient has been restored to physical health, or is at least still living. (Rumbold 1986, p.59)

However, Frankl (2004) does not regard meaninglessness as pathological: 'rather than being the sign and symptom of a neurosis, it is, I would say, the proof of one's humanness' (p.143). As such, the dis-ease commensurate to lack of meaning may be more related to the type of growth that the spiritual traditions term the *Dark Night of the Soul* (Kavanaugh 1989; Grof and Grof 1990).

With the emergence of palliative care as an independent medical discipline, hope has been increasingly recognised as significant for both nursing research and clinical practice (Herth 1990; Herth and Cutcliffe 2002). This significance has always been seen clinically directed (Dufault and Martocchio 1985). According to Herth and Cutcliffe (2002), having 'identified hope as an influence on effective coping during times of loss, suffering and uncertainty,' research is now focusing on how 'those individuals who are in the advanced stages of a terminal illness maintain or engender their hope?' (p.977). Interestingly, in the first published study to incorporate a longitudinal element, Herth (1990) identifies seven 'hope-fostering strategies' among her convenience sample of 30 terminally-ill adults. Top of her list is 'interpersonal connectedness', with her participants saying they wanted 'someone who shares in my journey and walks with me' and 'the feeling that the person is truly present with me' (p.1254), which contrasts with three hindrances to hope: abandonment and isolation, uncontrollable pain, and devaluation of personhood. Hope, as Herth's participants define it, 'is an inner power that facilitates the transcendence of the present situation and movement toward new awareness and enrichment of being' (p.1256). Herth's work concords with Yalom's experience (2008) when, writing about overcoming death terror through connection, he asserts: 'One can offer no greater service to someone facing death … than to offer him or her your sheer presence' (p.125).

As a palliative care chaplain working in a secular healthcare environment, Yalom's non-religious emphasis on connectivity is relevant to my context. There is a strand within the literature on hope in palliative care that pushes hope firmly into the next life. Herbert (2006) is merely typical when he defines hope as 'the *mysterious anticipation of the ultimate*' (p.24) (see also Cutcliffe and Herth 2002). However, recourse to theological categories risks foreclosing the offer of psychospiritual care to those who, for whatever reason, do not have a religious faith; and, as will become clear, it also fails to address Rumbold's third order of hope, in which a dying person acknowledges that extinction is an existential possibility. Following Epicurus, Yalom (2008) works with existential extinction as *the* possibility and he considers that the soul is 'mortal and perishes with the body' (p.79). For this reason, he offers to remain present and connected with those facing death.

As a palliative care chaplain, I approach caring for people who are dying from a different place than Yalom, and I bring to my work the resources of the spiritual traditions of Western Christianity that have formed me. However, like Yalom, I work in a secular environment, where I would find it difficult to describe many of those for whom I care as, in any traditional sense, religious. The chaplaincy wisdom of a previous generation, which encouraged the chaplain to 'exercise his (*sic*) sacramental ministry' with 'sensitive concern' as 'an important part of his whole expression of caring' (Autton 1968, p.46), is no longer as widely relevant as once it may have been. From my personal perspective, the challenge of spiritual care is to be a person – shaped and resourced by my particular spiritual formation – alongside souls who are living and dying within a secular (but not necessarily unspiritual) setting. The question that presses itself upon me, and I think many other chaplains, is how to do this in a way that is of benefit to a person who is dying. What for me is a personal challenge, also embodies the wider philosophical and political question of what spiritual care might be in a modern secular health service – another instance in which 'the personal is political'. The two questions are interrelated and in attempting directly to address the first, it is inevitable that this book will implicitly address the second.

An overview

This book has grown out of, and is therefore shaped by, a piece of research that I undertook as part of an MSc programme in Therapeutic Counselling, at the University of Greenwich. As such, it is informed by psychotherapeutic theory, which has directed my thinking around how chaplains work in their relationship with a dying person. Another theoretical frame would have been equally valid, and would have opened different possibilities and closed others. But as will become clear, seeing the chaplain's relationship with a dying person from the perspective of 'transference' seems to me to be a particularly fruitful and insufficiently considered way of beginning to understand this work.

I begin, in Chapter 1, with the 'critical incident' that triggered my study. Encountering Daniel, a man in his 20s, prompted me to question what it might mean to offer spiritual care to a person who is dying in a way that might help them face the inevitability of their death. This chapter draws on the work of Rumbold (1986), an Australian pastoral theologian, to identify a critical point in the development of hope, the point at which a dying person may either slip into despair or find their hope transformed into hopefulness. The chapter introduces what I call four 'moments' in a theory of *the chaplain as a hopeful presence*.

Chapter 2 examines the first 'moment', the idea of the chaplain as an *evocative presence*, and introduces the idea of 'transference', a phenomenon that characterises all human contact. Transference is observable in the way a person's thoughts, feelings and expectations, which rightly attach to someone from their early experience – a parent, an authority figure, a lover – are projected unconsciously and inappropriately onto a person in the present. Chaplains are intuitively aware that their presence evokes transferential projection and this chapter examines four possible outcomes of the transferences that are projected onto a chaplain. I develop the idea that when chaplains stay-*with* a negative transference, they demonstrate their preparedness to be in human contact with a person who is dying *no-matter-what*. I identify this as the point at which the relationship between a chaplain and a dying person can turn into something that has the potential to be creatively therapeutic.

Having accepted and worked with the person's transferential projection, the chaplain has the possibility of becoming an *accompanying presence*, the second 'moment'. Uniquely among healthcarers, as accompaniers, chaplains have no therapeutic aim or professional agenda; they do not accompany in order to do something-*to* or -*for* the person for whom they are caring so much as simply to be someone with them. Chapter 3 conceptualises being-*with* an other in terms of Heidegger's concept of 'dwelling': active engagement without any well-meant intention to manipulate. Such accompanying extends to accepting a dying person's right to die their own death in their own way, the way they need to die, rather than any kind of prescribed 'good death'.

Once established as an accompanier, a chaplain may become a *comforting presence*, comforting a dying soul in the word's original sense of 'to strengthen'. Chapter 4 develops the idea of 'spiritual comfort' in terms of the way some people find strength in the *presence* of the chaplain. Typically, chaplains are prepared to remain with the authenticity of the dying person's experience, often in a place *beyond* where words are effective.

Rather than having a particular set of interventions that are aimed at helping a dying person to find or retain hope, and thereby to avoid falling into despair, chaplains offer themselves as a being-*with* that may itself be a *hopeful presence*. Chapter 5 looks at how hope may be reconceptualised, counterintuitively, as 'hope in the present', and how, in the face of a terminal diagnosis, hope may become reconfigured by presence. In this chapter, I draw on Gabriel Marcel's (2010) idea of 'absolute' hope to develop the idea that the chaplain's presence may facilitate 'an overall stance towards life' that recognises the inevitable yet remains open to the possibility of experience.

From this, I suggest that spiritual care can be rethought in terms of *presence* and pose the obvious question: if presence is such a fundamentally important aspect of spiritual care, then what does it mean to be present to a person who knows they are dying? Chapter 6 tries to address this question by thinking about what it can mean for healthcarers to face the anxieties raised by working with a dying other.

Why I try no longer to see 'patients'

The phrase, 'a dying other', may sound clumsy and uncomfortable, but I have become increasingly uncomfortable with using the word 'patient' to describe those with whom I work. The term 'patient' (from the Latin 'to suffer or endure'), is very useful as a piece of shorthand. However, the difficulty with the term is that it designates people as the objects of medical care and knowledge. In another word, it medicalises people, positioning them in relation to 'expert' medical knowledge and fixes them in relation to their 'acquired vulnerability and dependency imposed by changing health circumstances' (Chochinov 2007, p.184). It seems to me that the word 'patient' is inappropriate for chaplains and anyone with a concern for spiritual care, which, whatever it might be, is about treating human people as human beings. My discomfort with the noun 'patient' has led me to using adjectival phrases that frequently do feel clumsy and uncomfortable. However, these phrases are an attempt to make clear that the 'person who is dying', the 'dying person', the 'dying other', are people like us – may well *be us* in a very few moments – and to close something of the gap the word 'patient' opens between healthcarers and 'those for whom we care'.

With thanks

I owe a debt of thanks to those from whom I have learnt so much during the time I have been working on the material in this book. Many people have helped me and taught me, mostly without realising the effect that they have had on me. The quietful insights of Sylvia Lindsay set me on a new path of spiritual growth; the generous introduction of Chris Cullen to Ram Dass, Thich Nhat Hanh and others from whom I have learnt so much, has been valuable beyond price; the model of hope development shared by Bruce Rumbold, in print and over dinner, kick-started my research.

I am of course grateful to my supervisors Quentin Stimpson, who guided my research at The University of Greenwich, and Rob Hart, who kept watch over my clinical practice. My passionate, frustrating, creative, annoying, inspiring and supportive colleagues in the Psychosocial and Spiritual Care Team have given me more than they know, especially Anne Cullen, the most enabling manager a jobbing chaplain could pray for.

I have received more than I have given to my Chaplaincy Team colleagues (former and present): Gail Partridge, Bernadette Junor, Mary Benton and Sally Horne; Sarah Cole, Brandy Martin, Andrew Coni and Gouri Preace; Janet McKenzie, Katharine Lankey, Ellen Farmer, Tania Lucas, Jan Harding and Geraldine Worthington.

I am particularly grateful to the anonymous chaplains who where generous with their time and, most especially, with the ideas that made this research viable, and to Princess Alice Hospice who part funded my study and provided the supportive environment that values both chaplaincy and research. I am indebted to the Hospice's ever-resourceful former librarian, Jan Brooman, who sourced obscure papers with grace.

However, my most obvious debt is to a group of people I am unable to thank: to Daniel, Elaine, the visitor in Room 20, Peter, Rosetta, Karl, Thomas, Joan, Arthur, Phoebe, Michael, Alfred, Sally, Yvonne, Ray, Penny, Sue and Chris, and all the other people whom I have had the privilege to care for and learn from.[1] To you, I am grateful.

Finally, to my wife Marion, you continue to be more understanding and patient than it is reasonable for me to expect. By your constant belief and unbounded love, you make me hopeful. For everything, thank you.

---

1   Through the book, I give vignettes of personal encounters with people that I have cared for. In every case, the names used are pseudonyms, except for the two vignettes of Karl and of Yvonne, where I have been given permission to use their real names.

Chapter 1

Hope Beyond Recovery

Daniel: My critical incident

There was a message on my voicemail: 'Daniel in Room 8 has asked to see a *male* social worker, and we all agreed that you should see him. Can you try and see him today?'

The hospice where I work has a strong social work team. It employs several full-time, or full-time equivalent, staff members, all of whom have extensive experience in a range of social work practices, some with counselling training, and the team is enhanced by additional part-time and administrative staff. As a team, these staff members deliver general social work support, as well as specialist bereavement care and psychological support. Yet in this situation, with all their experience, no one was able to offer what I had to offer, because none of them is male! In a professional world dominated by female colleagues, it is reassuring (to me at least) that there are still times when only a man will do!

So, as I went to see Daniel, I wondered how I might introduce myself. I turned over several possibilities and finally settled on something like, 'The Social Work Department said you'd like me to call'.

Daniel had, of course, been expecting me, and when I arrived he invited me in and asked his relatives to leave us together; and as he began to speak, hesitantly at first but directly, I began to wonder who it was that I was now that I was with him.

As far as I understood it, I wasn't exactly what I thought he thought I was. Daniel had asked for a *male* social worker. I might, by accident of birth, be *male*, but by choice I'm no social worker. I choose to be a chaplain – but that was not the choice of healthcare professional Daniel had made. So I wondered if I was being dishonest with him; or – which might be worse – whether I was being dishonest and professionally unethical with myself. I wondered whether he would send me away if he knew I was a chaplain in social work clothing; but if it wasn't me, who would be there? Would our hospice have looked outside for someone who had the dual credentials of maleness and social work qualification? Could we even have found such a person at short notice that would be willing and able to attend?

As I was turning these hypothetical cartwheels in the privacy of my own mind, Daniel continued to speak. And he voiced anxieties that, up to this point, he had been unable to share with his family: anxieties about his own gnawing sense that his treatment wasn't working; anxieties about the advisability of continuing with the treatment; anxieties about his deepening realisation that, as a young man, he was facing his premature end.

And as he spoke, my own realisations deepened about my unease at the basis of our relationship: Who was I with this young man? Who should I be? Whoever I was, our conversation seemed now to be turning me into his counsellor, and I wondered if his request for a *male* social worker been a coded request for a *male* counsellor.

I fantasised about how I might be if I were a *male* social worker. I would have used people skills developed over years of practice to facilitate Daniel to say what he felt he needed to say, but had so far been unable to say; I would have accepted him where he was, as he was; and I would have listened, actively and empathically.

I fantasised about how I might be if I were a *male* counsellor. I would have used people skills developed over years of practice to facilitate Daniel to say what he felt he needed to say, but had so far been unable to say; I would have accepted him where he was, as he was; and I would have listened, actively and empathically.

And I fantasised about how he might be if he knew I was a *male* chaplain. He might not have wanted my people skills developed over years of practice that might have facilitated him to say what he felt he needed to say, but had so far been unable to say. He might have thought I would not have accepted him where he was, as he was, and that I would not so much have listened, actively and empathically, as spoken about … well, who knows what it is that chaplains are supposed to speak about?

And as my realisations deepened that I was uncomfortable not knowing who I was, and as I fantasised about who and how I might be, something about this young man cut through my introspection and drew, no, pulled me into his world in a way I had not expected nor had I experienced before. As he told me that he felt the drugs weren't working and as he said, without saying, that he knew he was dying, something touched me with the presence of the dying he was living.

I had, of course, heard many other people tell me very similar things before. I have listened actively and, I hope, empathically to what they have said. I have sat with them in their painful anticipation of their loss. Sometimes (when appropriate) I have prayed with them; usually, I have left with an offer to return tomorrow. Often I have felt some kind of satisfaction that I had done something helpful; increasingly I have known that, at that base level where it truly mattered, I have been unconnected from their reality, untouched and unable to touch. Typically, I have then gone to a committee meeting, or coffee with a colleague, or lunch; or read an article about spiritual care, or prepared a talk for nurses; or I have done one of the many routine activities that are part of every chaplain's week.

But it was different with Daniel: somehow he had compelled me into his existential reality, and somehow I felt something of the un-walk-away-able reality of the present he was living. I was aware that, in a few moments, I would leave him; that I would go for that coffee or read that article, that maybe I would go home and kiss my wife, or whatever. But in a way I had not grasped before, in a place beyond the obvious and superficial, I sensed something of Daniel's not-going-anywhere experience, and with it, the all pervading awareness that, if he did go somewhere, he'd be taking his dying and his pain along with him.

I saw Daniel awakening to the full realisation that there was only one way through his situation, and his awakening to his truth awoke something in me to the truth of who I was with him in the few moments we had together.

I was not a *male* social worker – how could I be? But nor was I a *male* chaplain – although I was both. Least of all was I a *male* counsellor. I was one of two scared people sitting in a room together. I had gone in scared that I might not be what Daniel needed or wanted; scared that he might see through me and send me away. But while I was with him, I began to touch some of his scared-ness, and the longer we were together the more I seemed to feel his scared-ness. Towards the end of our brief time, and for a fragile breath, I became mindfully present to the intensity of a life lived towards death, and the overwhelming sadnesses of its premature losses.

It wore me out.

After I left Daniel, I needed coffee *and* a kiss from my wife. Later, I learned that Daniel had known all along that I was a chaplain, and that actually *he didn't care* (Nolan 2008a).

Before meeting Daniel, I had carelessly entertained the idea that I was more or less skilled in empathising with people who are dying; I was, after all, a hospice chaplain. But in those few, intense moments with Daniel, as he lived what Levinas describes as the 'impossibility of retreat' (Levinas 1969, cited in Cohen 2006, p.28) and what Heidegger terms 'the possibility ... *which is not to be outstripped*' (Heidegger 1962, p.294), the shallow naivety of my self-awareness was exposed. Through Daniel, I became aware that what I had previously mistaken as the courage to be *in extremis* with a dying other was in fact just an elaborate cover up: pretending to myself that I was okay with being around dying people, I was covering up my detached, inauthentic average everyday 'being-*towards*-death' (*Sein zum Tode*, Heidegger 1962, pp.277–311). As Heidegger puts it, 'In inappropriate certainty, that of which one is certain is held covered up' (Heidegger 1962, p.301). My naïve certainty about being around a dying other was exposed as nothing more than the inappropriate cover for my deep-rooted anxiety about death, which is my impending certainty – as it is ours. My misplaced certainty was but one more 'everyday failing evasion *in the face of* death [that is] an *inauthentic* being-*towards*-death' (Heidegger 1962, p.303).

Several important things emerged for me from this awareness, not the least of which was the realisation that, if I was to continue in this work and maintain any idea of being effective in it, then I needed to confront my own fear of death; my personal death anxiety, my own private thanatophobia (Cooper and Adams 2005; Yalom 1980). Yet being with Daniel as he stared his death anxiety full in the face (Yalom 2008) and watching him begin the process of letting go of his hope for recovery, I felt helpless and I was left wondering how my being-*with* him could have been therapeutic.

The development of hope: Rumbold's 'three orders'

Around the time I met Daniel, I had been invited to write a short article on hope (Nolan 2009a). Researching the article, I came across Rumbold's (1986) model of hope development (Figure 1.1 see p.35), which he develops from Weisman's (1972) psychiatric description of the defences dying people deploy to protect themselves against the anxieties aroused by the impending certainty, which is their death. In his account, Weisman describes 'three orders' of denial: denying the facts of the illness, i.e. the symptoms; denying what the symptoms *mean*; and denying the possibility of death as the end of existence. Weisman observes that each denial has its own corresponding level of acceptance and as each order of denial breaks down, as the denial becomes impossible to sustain, the person who is dying begins to accept something of the new reality in which they are living; a new reality which is itself limited by the new order of denial. Rumbold extends Weisman's account to suggest that hope is, by definition, always associated with, and sustained by, denial and acceptance.

First-order: Denial of symptoms and hope for recovery

When a person first begins to experience symptoms that they find disturbing, and perhaps may even suspect to be serious, they frequently and very understandably react by denying the significance of what appears to be happening to them. In this way, people often ignore worrying symptoms or interpret them as something less concerning. For example, writing about her experience of living with multiple myeloma, diagnosed in 2006, Pat Wade describes how she lived 'in denial' for almost two years:

> Over the preceding 20 months, reduced mobility and crippling bone pain had become part of my everyday life. As I could not identify the cause and, because being incapacitated was not part of my ageing plan, I stubbornly persisted in denying the existence of a problem. Unconsciously, my verbal and body language conveyed a

strong message that the subject of my health was off the
agenda of observational comment and discussion. Few
had the courage to cross this barrier to the truth: that I
wasn't doing well. (Wade 2010, pp.17–18)

It is important to recognise that denial has its value and, as humans,
we do derive significant psychological benefit from denying
certain aspects of our experience. Denial is the psychological
mechanism of blocking from awareness something that we perceive
to be threatening and, as such, denial provides a worried person
with psychic protection from the unpleasant effects of their own
anxieties. In this way, denial enables us to continue functioning
more or less normally in situations in which we may otherwise feel
overwhelmed. Because of this, an attempt to try to compel another
person to surrender the sense of relative safety that they derive from
their denial and so step, prematurely, into the harsh reality of their
impending certainty is an act of psychological abuse. As Levine
(1986) puts it, stealing denial is a maleficent act that healthcarers
should resist, no matter how much they feel that the person for
whom they are caring needs to face up to reality (p.163).

When a person is 'in denial', hope is not needed. As Rumbold
puts it:

When first-order denial operates there is no place for
hope in the face of illness and death. We see ourselves
as healthy, and we cannot contemplate a change in that
situation; in essence we think of ourselves as immortal.
(Rumbold 1986, p.62)

However, the limitations of this initial, 'first-order denial' – what
Nekolaichuk and Bruera (1998) term the 'myth of immortality'
(p.37) – are obvious and potentially life-threatening. As a result,
denial can – and often does – seriously delay a sick person seeking
or accepting treatment.

Nonetheless, as symptoms progress, first-order denial becomes
increasingly difficult to sustain and, under normal circumstances,
the phantasy on which the denial is founded breaks down. As Pat
Wade explains:

> Suppressing the reality, however, resulted in displaced irrational bursts of anger and irritation. These were at odds with the serenity that I usually presented to the world. I was not coping, but fear weakened my power of logic. Privately, I attributed the pain to over-indulgent exercise and convinced myself that the symptoms must be psychosomatic and therefore 'would be fine tomorrow'. That tomorrow never came. (Wade 2010, p.18)

It is at this point, when the first-order denial fails and the seriously ill person begins to acknowledge their symptoms and accept their need for help, that what Rumbold (1986) terms first-order hope starts to emerge as 'a hope for recovery, a hope for a return to our former state of health. At this point no other possibilities are envisaged' (p.62). According to Rumbold, first-order hope may emerge out of a period of despair following the breakdown of first-order denial, or there may be a straightforward transition from admitting the reality of illness to affirming a *hope for recovery*. In either case, the transition is delicate and admitting illness may actually plunge a person who is seriously ill into a despair and resignation from which they do not emerge (p.63).

Second-order: Denial of non-recovery and hope beyond recovery

When it emerges, first-order *hope for recovery* finds its support in a second-order denial – *denial of non-recovery*. As Pat Wade relates:

> When faced with a stem cell transplant in May 2007, I was promised 'remission'. My initial reaction was suspicion and cynicism. However, once remission became a reality, euphoria set in. I began to deny the possibility of myeloma relapse. I went from month-to-month resuming and enjoying purposeful activity. Despite the challenge of transport systems to a person with impaired mobility, I recklessly travelled the world alone to sport conventions as though there was no tomorrow. I swam a marathon for charity, took up exercise for disabled and was liberated from home confinement through acquisition of an electric 'buggy'. (Wade 2010, p.19)

As Rumbold observes, whereas medical staff and the sick person's family and close friends are likely to have confronted and discouraged the first-order denial, second-order denial – described by Nekolaichuk and Bruera (1998) as the 'myth of the magic bullet' (pp.37–8) – is actively supported. According to Rumbold (1986), second-order denial is encouraged, precisely 'because it gives medical access to the symptoms while suppressing fear of death and the difficult questions which attend that fear' (p.63). And yet, however necessary such support and encouragement may be in order for a sick person to engage with treatment, the potential for disappointment and increased despair is obvious.

Rumbold describes the well-intentioned collusion of family and friends (and perhaps some healthcare professionals) who, in an effort to keep the sick person's thoughts and attitudes positive and hopeful, may try to control or manipulate the information they receive. Nonetheless, the unintended consequence of this may be that the sick person's 'attempts to test reality will give misleading, or at least ambiguous, results' (p.63). Consequently, if active treatment is withdrawn, this well-intentioned collusion may actually deepen the sense of abandonment and betrayal experienced by the one they are trying to help, fuelling their anger and, perversely, increasing their risk of falling into despair. As Rumbold acknowledges:

> Our social preference for second-order denial linked with first-order hope means that *the breakdown of second-order denial is the critical transition* if hope is to continue to develop in terminal illness. (Rumbold 1986, p.63, emphasis added)

For hope to continue developing, Rumbold argues, and so become hope beyond mere insistence on recovery, the possibilities for dying need to be faced and explored. Yet the social support that had previously buoyed hope of recovery may now begin to work against the person who is terminally-ill, disallowing them the freedom they need to contemplate dying as part of their hope. The tragedy is that lack of support at this point may mean that any acceptance, which might be emerging as the denial breaks down, results in resignation and despair, since 'the withdrawal of community is particularly destructive of hope' (p.63).

The breakdown of second-order *denial of non-recovery* is, indeed, the critical transition, the point where a dying person must navigate their way between the related poles of hope (Latin: *sperare*) and despair (Latin: *desperare*). As Rumbold observes, this critical transition is the point at which, 'If all our hope has been invested in recovery, then that hope may virtually be destroyed by the new perception of second-order acceptance' (p.63). It was at this point of critical transition that I met Daniel; at this point, his *denial of non-recovery* was breaking down visibly and the emergence of any *hope beyond recovery* was at best insecure and uncertain; at this point, he was at risk of falling into despair. Rumbold's point is that, in order to secure the second-order *hope beyond recovery*, it is important that a person who is making the critical transition has the opportunity to talk honestly *and know that they are being heard*. For Rumbold, second-order hope may take form as a realistic hope to die; but, while most 'terminally-ill people do seem to reach this second stage where such a hope becomes possible … those who can find a meaningful hope which they are allowed to affirm are distressingly few' (p.64).

Of course, not everyone will get to, or will want to get to this point of critical transition. However, if there is to be any chance of finding second-order *hope beyond recovery*, a person who is dying needs to be allowed to face and explore (at least to some degree) the reality of their lived experience. The problem is that the habit of well-intentioned collusion becomes difficult to break, and the dying person's close friends and family, and perhaps even their medical team, may struggle to permit them to say what they need to say.

> A somewhat tentative statement such as, 'If I do have to go at least I hope it will be as peaceful as it was for old Bill last night' is more than likely to be met with the response, 'Don't be morbid' than with the recognition that here is a person beginning to explore possibilities for his own dying. (Rumbold 1986, p.64)

As Rumbold observes, the first-order hopes, established through the period of treatment, can crush the second-order hopes that begin to emerge as a person accepts that treatment is no longer an option and that they are dying (p.64).

When it is allowed to be expressed, second-order *hope beyond recovery* is likely to be a more short-term, more 'realistic' hope than *hope for recovery*; it is also likely to be a more varied hope than the single-minded *hope for recovery*. *Hope beyond recovery* may simply be hope:

> to die with dignity;
> for the continuing success of children;
> that a partner will find the support they need;
> that their life's contribution will continue and be found useful.
> (Rumbold 1986, p.64)

For Elaine, *hope beyond recovery* meant, at least in part, that she would not die angry.

Elaine: Moving on from angry

When I first met Elaine, I was unprepared for her frankness. She spoke openly about how she had only recently been told that her illness was terminal. She had been ill for two and a half years, but she said that, even so, she was surprised how shocked she felt at being given a terminal diagnosis. '

There were the inevitable "Why?" questions', she said. 'Why have I been struck down with this thing? But actually, I haven't asked that question much, which has surprised me. I was angry ... very angry – angry at the world; and that's not me. I'm not like that. I'm usually very calm. That's not the way I want to be. I think that's a quite natural reaction, but I don't want to be angry; I don't want to die angry. But actually, I feel as if I'm moving on from that now. I feel as if I'm moving into trying to making sense of what is ahead.'

I felt myself coveting Elaine's hard-won wisdom. I wanted to know how Elaine had got to this point; was there something she had learned from her experience that I could share with others?

'Is that "making sense" a kind of thinking through questions,' I asked. 'Or is it a process; a coming to maturity about things?'

'Yes, it's thinking through questions maturely. I suppose you see a lot of this.'

'I see a lot of people in similar situations, but – and this sounds trite – everyone goes through this on their own. This is your journey; and you have to do it in your own way.'

'That's the difficulty I have. I don't have anyone … Actually, there is one person I met at my oncology clinic who is terminally-ill, but she's not as advanced as I am. We talk about things, but you think you're going mad. There's no way really to know that what you're going through is normal.'

Elaine spoke about how, after hearing her diagnosis was terminal, she experienced a withdrawal into her close family unit.

'What you describe sounds quite natural to me,' I suggested. 'Like when you have a physical shock your systems withdraw to protect your vital functions.'

'That's how we described it. The closest analogy we could find was when an animal is injured it goes off alone to hide, to lick its wounds and hopefully emerge stronger. That's the closest we could get to what was happening.'

'And what that suggests is that you can trust your instincts. Your instinctive response is okay.'

She looked across to her husband. 'Our instincts have been a pretty good guide.'

I had stayed long enough for Elaine and, as I prepared to leave, Elaine suggested that I could call by each day, see how she was and maybe have a chat for 10 minutes or so.

I tried several times to return to Elaine, but always managed to arrive at an inconvenient moment. Finally, the day before she was due to be discharged, I managed to see her. Initially, we 'chit-chatted', and then she spoke about her illness.

'It's predestined. That's what I believe.'

'Is it?' I couldn't accept this for a second, but it wasn't my place to challenge Elaine.

'Yes. I have to. If I didn't believe that I'd go mad. There has to be some meaning in it. I know there was a reason why we couldn't have children. I can see that now. It's because I wouldn't have to be saying "Goodbye" to them. I don't know how anyone can do that. So there will be a reason. I might not see it, but there will be one. If there wasn't then I'd be so angry that I'd get a shotgun and shoot everyone! No … that's just the anger. I don't want to be angry. It's not a good way to be. Not at this time of my life. I was angry, but I've moved on from that. I want to be at peace.'

Again, I felt my covetousness rising: I hadn't yet gleaned her wisdom, so I asked about moving on from the anger.

'What helps that?'

'What helps that? That's a good question. What helps that? Prayer helps that. I'm not very good at it. Or maybe I am good at it. I asked to be saved when I had my bad time in January, and I'm still here – so maybe I *am* good at it. He did what I wanted, although then I got angry because I couldn't do what *I* wanted. Bugger!' She smiled. 'But I am glad now.'

'Just for the record!'

'Yes!' Her smile broadened. 'Being calm. When you know you haven't got long, you want to live your life to the full. People say that they're living life to the full, but life passes you by. I lived at a cracking pace, and it's nice to do things, to watch the telly or meet people or read a paper. But it's important just to be. When I saw the heron this morning, it wasn't just a case of, "Oh! There's a heron!" and back to reading the paper. I went out there and watched it, I *drank* it in. Now I have a lovely memory of it imprinted in me.'

Once more, Elaine was tiring. She told me that she wouldn't say goodbye ('I'm not very good with goodbyes, at the moment') and said that she had expressed her wish to be here (in the Hospice) 'when the time comes'.

Sometime later, Elaine returned for symptom control. 'You're looking a lot better,' I ventured.

'I feel a lot better. I've been given a prognosis now of weeks, but I'm okay with that. I'm much less angry than when I came in last time. I've had a few visitors, and it's quite tiring. I've said this to you before, but it's like you feel you have to entertain them. You almost have to fill in the gaps in the conversation. It's a bit much when you're feeling bad. I've got some more coming tomorrow.'

'You're seeing visitors then?'

'Yes! That's a change from last time. It's that the anger has gone. I've worked through a lot of stuff while I was at home. I'm seeing the ones that I won't see again. That will leave just my little group, my little group of people I want to be with me until the end of my life.'

I felt I was getting close to discovering something of what Elaine knew. 'How did you get there?'

'By going over things. We talked about a lot of things. This is the way it is going to be and there's no use fighting it. We'd rather things were going to be different, but they're not.'

'This is putting it a bit crudely, but it sounds like you've changed your mind.'

'Yes! That's exactly it. There's no point in being angry; it takes up so much energy. I know I'm going to be on a gradual, slow decline now, so I have to get on with it. My body is getting weaker, but I feel emotionally stronger. I hope I will.'

Elaine was tired, and I took my leave. I didn't speak with her again.

Elaine realised her hope not to die angry and she was helped in that by the honesty of her husband, who allowed her the freedom she needed to 'talk about a lot of things'. Like Elaine, he wanted things to be different; but like Elaine, he knew they would not be, and despite his pain he found it within himself to allow Elaine to say what she needed to say, to talk honestly, to know *that she was being heard* and so to make her critical transition.

Third-order: Hope that faces existential extinction

According to Rumbold (1986), despite being more short-term and more 'realistic', second-order *hope beyond recovery* is itself supported by a third-order denial: 'the possibility that death will be the end for us has not yet really been faced' (p.64). Rumbold's point is, not that people who are dying should be encouraged to give up their hope of surviving death, or indeed that those who do acknowledge 'the possibility that death will be the end' will then cease to believe in a life hereafter. His point is that *hope beyond recovery* has the capacity for still further development into a *hope that accepts the existential possibility of extinction at death, but that nevertheless finds a sense of ultimate meaning in the life that has been lived.* This 'mature hope', Rumbold argues, is based not on denial but is 'supported and validated by memory'; it is a hope 'which can examine all possibilities' and then 'choose what will be hoped for' (p.65). Such hope is a hope that may hope to survive death, but it does so 'in full recognition that it is a faith claim, not an unarguable certainty' (p.65).

Not everyone will develop a mature, third-order hope, and nor is Rumbold suggesting that everyone should be expected to – he is certainly not advocating that anyone should in any way be compelled to. I do not know whether Elaine developed a mature, third-order hope: she did fulfil her hope not to die angry, which she could do because she was able to negotiate the critical transition around the breakdown of her second-order *denial of non-recovery*.

The point of critical transition was the point at which I met Daniel, the point at which he stared his death anxiety full in the face and the point that posed me the question of how my being-*with* him might have been therapeutic. This book represents an account of the findings of my researches with spiritual caregivers, chaplains working in palliative care settings in hospices and hospitals in southeast England. Over a period of eight months, between December 2008 and August 2009, as part of an MSc in Therapeutic Counselling, at The University of Greenwich, I interviewed 20 palliative care chaplains who between them had in excess of 100 years' experience in offering spiritual care to people who are dying. The question I was interested in answering was:

> How do palliative care chaplains counsel terminally-ill people who are surrendering their now redundant *hope for recovery* and negotiating the critical transition that avoids slipping into despair?

Using a Grounded Theory approach, what emerged from the data gathered from unstructured individual interviews and group work, was that the relationship between a palliative care chaplain and a dying person has the potential to move through a series of what I term developmental 'moments' that are characterised by the quality of the chaplain's presence or being-*with* the other. I will describe these four 'moments' or modes of presence – 'evocative presence'; 'accompanying presence'; 'comforting presence'; and 'hopeful presence' – in the following chapters, but I want to be very clear about what I see as an important point.

As an aspect of contemporary healthcare, spiritual care is a misunderstood and disputed practice. In large part, this is because it is closely associated with the religious traditions, which in turn is due to the emergence of spiritual care within Western Christianity (Swift 2009). Despite strong claims by some that it is the responsibility of healthcarers in general and nurses in particular to deliver spiritual care (McSherry 2001; 2006), not all do and not all see it as their responsibility (Paley 2008a; Walter 1997). In my experience, all healthcarers are *not* able to attend to the spiritual needs of those in their care, either because they lack training or inclination, or both. I would argue that, while all healthcarers have the potential *to contribute* to the spiritual care of sick and dying people, claiming that *anyone* can deliver spiritual care serves to devalue the specialist nature of that care. Spiritual care, whatever else it may be, is fundamentally relational. I would argue that those healthcarers who offer their care *relationally* are able to offer spiritual care. But I would also argue that those who struggle to care relationally can, nevertheless learn skills of care that contribute to the spiritual support of those in their care.

The model of spiritual care that I am describing in this book is, then, a model that is particular to the kind of specialist spiritual care that chaplains, by virtue of the specifics of their role, are able to offer. It is a model that, in my experience and practice, has integrity with its origins within the traditions of religion and which continues to have relevance in a secular, even post-religious context. It is a model that describes what chaplains *do*, but that contains lessons for those healthcarers who offer their care *relationally*.

Development of hope in terminal illness

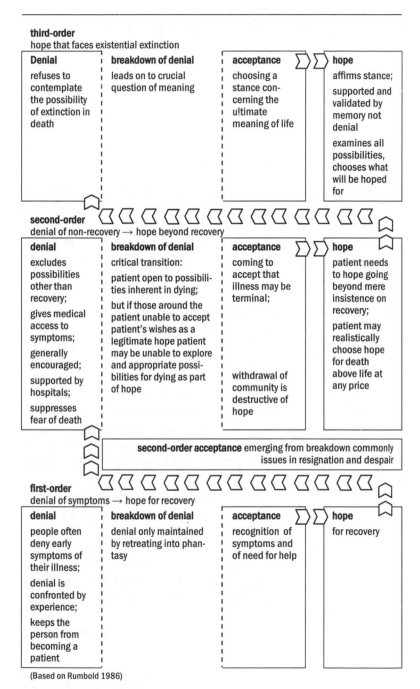

third-order
hope that faces existential extinction

Denial	breakdown of denial	acceptance	hope
refuses to contemplate the possibility of extinction in death	leads on to crucial question of meaning	choosing a stance concerning the ultimate meaning of life	affirms stance; supported and validated by memory not denial
			examines all possibilities, chooses what will be hoped for

second-order
denial of non-recovery → hope beyond recovery

denial	breakdown of denial	acceptance	hope
excludes possibilities other than recovery;	critical transition:	coming to accept that illness may be terminal;	patient needs to hope going beyond mere insistence on recovery;
gives medical access to symptoms;	patient open to possibilities inherent in dying;		
generally encouraged;	but if those around the patient unable to accept patient's wishes as a legitimate hope patient may be unable to explore and appropriate possibilities for dying as part of hope		patient may realistically choose hope for death above life at any price
supported by hospitals;		withdrawal of community is destructive of hope	
suppresses fear of death			

second-order acceptance emerging from breakdown commonly issues in resignation and despair

first-order
denial of symptoms → hope for recovery

denial	breakdown of denial	acceptance	hope
people often deny early symptoms of their illness;	denial only maintained by retreating into phantasy	recognition of symptoms and of need for help	for recovery
denial is confronted by experience;			
keeps the person from becoming a patient			

(Based on Rumbold 1986)

Figure 1.1 Rumbold's 'three orders'
Reproduced from Watson, et al. (2009), with permission

Chapter 2

Evocative Presence

A visitor in Room 20: 'And ... ?'

In the morning handover, the man in Room 20 had been described as someone whose lifestyle could present complications for the way the nursing staff would care for him. The words 'drug abuse' had been mooted and I thought I should perhaps visit him as a priority to see if I could establish the beginnings of a supportive relationship.

When I arrived at his room, the door was wide open and he looked as if he was asleep. However, I could see there was a woman with him (I thought she might be his wife) and I decided I would try to get to know some of his family. I knocked and walked in.

'Hello, I've come to introduce myself. My name's Steve, I'm the chaplain here.'

The woman looked at me, but said nothing. She had no need to speak; the silent indifference in her eyes was more eloquent than any words she might have used. Her debilitating look froze me at a distance and, although my body was already halfway into the room, it was as though her wordless interrogation was preventing me from joining it: 'And ... ?'

I felt the powerful emptiness of her silent stare as a direct and simple challenge. It was as though she was demanding, 'What *possible* use could you be to us at this time?'

It wasn't that she was angry – at least, not angry with me – she was just indifferent ... *aggressively* indifferent. I was of no consequence to her; I had nothing to offer, she could see no value in me ... and just how long was I going to stand there, intrusively wondering what next to say?

My only thoughts in that moment were to review the ways that I could say a face-saving 'Goodbye'!

Although there was only her and me, and the sleeping form by which she was standing, I felt exposed – as exposed as if we had been on a public stage and I had offered my hand, only to be indignantly ignored. I understood her message; she had spoken clearly enough, and I made my retreat.

Sometimes the obvious is so obvious that to point it out seems too predictable and too banal. But in thinking about a chaplain's presence, perhaps the most obvious, predictable and banal thing to point out is that it is always an embodied presence: that is to say, a chaplain, like any other healthcarer, is first of all another body in the room. However, a chaplain's body is never just *a* body, it is always a *particular* body. Tall or short; female or male; dark or light; older or younger; thin or not so: chaplains come in a very wide range of models, each complete with their own personal history, set of relationships, beliefs, values and tastes, and abilities to cope.

Chaplains, all chaplains, are individuals – that much is obvious. However, once a chaplain has identified herself as a *chaplain*, she has opened herself to the risk of being stripped of the particularities that make her the specific individual she is – Karen, aged 43, from south London, a Methodist minister with a partner, two teenage boys and a mother recently admitted to hospital with suspected osteoporosis; a former advertising buyer who plays jazz clarinet, loves sailing and who has recently developed troubling doubts about the Resurrection, for example. Identifying oneself as a chaplain opens the possibility of being reduced to the archetype of 'the Vicar', a character who has limited interests, which in the main are to do with God, religion and going to church. The same phenomenon is, of course, apparent among other healthcarers, particularly among social workers, whose specialist traits are often assumed to include their ability to interfere in another person's business in inverse proportion that person's particular desire to be helped. Doctors and nurses – the latter being frequently mistaken for 'angels' – similarly risk being stripped of their individual identity and permitted to exist only as an archetype.

In retrospect, I suspect that this is what the woman visiting in Room 20 did with me. Walking through the door, I might have been anyone; more to the point, I might have been someone she perceived as being of some use to her at that particular point of her need. However, in the moment that I named myself and said 'I'm the chaplain here', I became for her an archetype – 'the Vicar' – an individual for whom she could perceive no use because, as far as she understood things, 'vicars' have little or nothing to offer to people like her and the man she was standing with: in short, people who are not church-goers. The fact that, actually, I am not a vicar was a technical point, an irrelevant detail. That I had identified myself as a member of the religious class was enough to parade my irrelevance to her and to license her rejection of me and my like. I might have anticipated a more open welcome from Peter.

Peter: How now to pray?

'The last person who prayed for me in hospital was a nun. She said, "You shouldn't expect to be healed; miracles don't happen these days, they were just for the time of the Bible." If that's the way you're going to pray for me, you can walk out the door right now, because that's not the kind of prayer I'm interested in!'

I'd felt on edge with Peter almost from before I'd entered his room. The handover sheet indicated his religion innocuously as 'Christian' and I imagined that this presaged a conservative faith. I envisaged someone who was probably more than usually committed to beliefs that were likely seasoned with a hint of intolerance towards other beliefs. I imagined this because, in an early part of my own life, I was that man – the liberal perspective I now have has had a tortuous gestation, but I remembered that my earlier me would have, at best, been suspicious of the present me and, creating Peter in the image of my earlier me, I fancied that, at best, he would be suspicious of the present me and, at worst, he would simply reject me.

The man I met did seem guarded. I introduced myself and said I was the chaplain, and unlike so many of those who speak about the trajectory of their illness, he gave me his testimony.

'I'm believing the promises of God,' he told me. 'God tells us that "by his stripes we are healed" and that his promises are "new every morning", and I'm living by those promises.'

I imagined how some of my colleagues might have heard this affirmation: 'The gentleman in Room 24 has good support from his family and his church, but we think he is in denial.'

He may well have been 'in denial', but his strong statement about holding on to the promises of God seemed to be more about remaining faithful to how he understood his God than about closing his mind to the possibility that he was in fact dying, and dying quite quickly. Nonetheless, I noticed that I too was guarded. I was aware of feeling that if he suspected I was a 'liberal' I would confirm his sense that institutionalised religion, in the form of a chaplain, was antithetical to what he described as his 'non-denominational' beliefs and that betraying my faith perspective would leave him spiritually isolated.

So I measured my responses, consciously examining each sentence, almost each word, to gauge whether they might be both acceptable to him and authentic to me. I've become quite proud of being theologically bi-lingual. Having lived and moved in and among a number of theological persuasions – Roman Catholic, charismatic, neo-Pentecostal, evangelical, Baptist, liberal, radical – I like to feel that I have more than a working understanding of a variety of Christian sub-traditions; that I can understand their various mindsets and linguistic nuances.

I felt guarded and yet it was I who made the offer to pray. Maybe it would have been 'safer' to have got to know him a little and left it at that, leaving the way open for me to come back and develop a trusting relationship.

Peter accepted my offer and, as I moved to sit closer to him, he told me about his earlier experience with the nun.

How now to pray?

I didn't feel I could pray with any amount of integrity for Peter to get better. But clearly I couldn't pray that he would be realistic about his prognosis. Rightly or wrongly, I decided with myself that 'healing' was an ambiguous enough word for me to be able to use it in my prayer; it seemed to me that each of us could load this word with the meaning we wanted – or needed – and that I'd let God make up his own mind! At least I felt I'd wriggled off the hook on to which I'd skewered myself.

Peter seemed to accept my prayer, so I took my leave.

I made a point of seeing him again the next day.

I'd hoped to build on what I thought we had begun to establish, and it seemed to be going okay until, explaining the composition of our chaplaincy team, I mentioned that one member had a Sufi background.

'What's that?'

'Well it comes out of Islam. She herself was brought up Roman Catholic, but she has learnt a lot from the mystical tradition of Sufism.'

The look in Peter's eyes was enough to tell me I'd said the wrong thing, but if I was in any doubt, his commentary made it clear: 'Oh that's awful.'

'Awful.'

'I suppose you have to do that, to be politically correct, but do you not think it's a bad thing to involve other religions?'

'Actually, she's very good; she spends time with people, listening to them and helping them spiritually.'

'But do you not think you should be trying to help people find salvation? Do you not find that people, when they're getting close to the end want help to find God?'

'Actually, it's not my job to try to change what people believe. My job is to support people in the way that they need.'

'But do you not think that people need to find God before they pass on?'

'Well, I might think that, but it's not for me to try to put what I believe on to someone else.'

I'd blown my cover! And, although I tried to rebuild something, it was obvious that I was too much of a 'liberal'. Despite my quiet conceit at my theological bi-linguality, it was highly unlikely that I was ever going to be able to offer spiritual care to Peter; we were just too far apart.

Perhaps I had been wrong to try. In my defence, it was not too unreasonable to suppose that I might be able to communicate with someone who was living in a world of belief that I had come from; but then I knew that the person I had been would have been suspicious of the type of person that I have become. I would have reduced me to an archetype, which would have evoked a particular kind of response in me.

The chaplain as an 'evocative presence'

Although many, if not most, of the chaplains in my research group lacked a technical term for the phenomenon of being stripped of their individuality and assigned the role of religious archetype, they intuitively recognised and identified with the experience. One chaplain told me about the way in which the details of his physical presence, which he described as that of a 'rather formal looking, religious gentleman' (CHP001.42)[2], evoked a response in one particular woman he visited:

> When I turned up at her bedside she was very emotional, she wanted to cry. And I … obviously, very gently, tried to go down the road of trying to find out what that was about, and why I evoked those tears in her. I don't think it was – for some people it's sometimes guilt … I don't think with her it was quite that. It was more wistful, it was more nostalgic; it was more a sense of loss. (CHP001.05)

His sense was that his physical presence, as a 'rather formal looking, religious gentleman', and the sacrament that he brought to this woman evoked in her a certain religious nostalgia:

> I came back with communion and this – the sacrament – actually was, I think, a way in which she was … taken back to something that was clearly very important to her as a girl. And she was able to, well, to reconnect, I think would be the right way to put that; you know, she had, as it were, some residual faith, and her encounter with me was, you know, it very much evoked that for her. (CHP001.05)

This chaplain was clear: there was something about his encounter with the woman he visited that had evoked a response in her, and that this 'something', which was typical of many of his encounters with those he visited, was more to do with his *presence* than anything he might have said to them:

> She was typical of a certain kind of encounter that I have with terminally-ill people – this sense that they do have a kind of residual faith somewhere. I talk in terms of it being like a very deep well, which might, or which perhaps undoubtedly does have some cool water at the bottom of it, and I'm as it were, you know, the link

---

2   The CHP codes relate to participants in the research project, base data for whom (age, gender, religion, ordination status, and years' experience) are detailed in the Appendix.

between them and the water at the bottom of the well. I
help them, I think, by my presence as much as anything
else – as much as by anything that I might say – to access
that. (CHP001.05)

While chaplains may not have a technical term for what I am calling
their 'evocative presence', counsellors and psychotherapists know
this phenomenon as transference/countertransference. Not all
writers are convinced by the concept of transference (Rogers 2004,
pp.198–218), perhaps in part because it originates with Freud and
psychoanalysis. However, as Watts, Nye and Savage (2002) observe,
clergy and other caring professionals 'find themselves the object of
strong attitudes and quite intense emotions' (p.262), which could
be described as irrational to the extent that some of those they care
for think 'they are marvellous while others are highly critical of
them' (p.262). Writing for Christian ministers, Watts et al. explain
that:

> The concept of transference implies that feelings or
> attitudes that belong to a significant past relationship are
> transferred onto the relationship with the … carer. The
> two key hallmarks are feelings that are a repetition of
> the past, and inappropriate to the present. (Watts et al.
> 2002, p.262)

Watts et al. acknowledge that, outside psychoanalysis, transference
is an under-researched area, and they comment that because clergy
(and by extension chaplains) are 'generally much better known
as people than are analysts they are perhaps less vulnerable to
transference relationships, though these may still arise' (p.262).
They go on to observe that:

> Though the psychoanalytic tradition assumes that intense
> emotional reactions to analysts or other carers arise from
> the transference of feelings from significant problematic
> relationships in the past, this may not be the only way in
> which they can do so. There may be more general aspects
> of how emotionally needy people relate to those that try
> to care for them that give rise to intense feelings. Strong
> emotional dependence can give rise to idealisation of the

carer, based in part on gratitude for the extent to which emotional needs are met. On the other hand, there can be anger and frustration at emotional needs not being fully met, and perhaps also resentment at being heavily dependent on another person. (Watts *et al.* 2002, p.262)

Whatever we call this phenomenon, Hinksman (1999), writing on pastoral counselling, observes that the 'religious matrix' in which chaplains operate may mobilise what Jung terms an 'archetypal transference':

In such an instance, in addition to the complications of transference and countertransference, there are the quasi-magical and other-worldly expectations which are not so much to do with the counsellee's expectations of another person but of whatever transcendent elements the counsellee associates with the counsellor or the counsellor's provenance. (Hinksman 1999, p.101)

The point is that the presence of a chaplain will evoke a response that is more to do with what the chaplain unconsciously represents for the person they are visiting than with who the chaplain is in herself. In other words, people relate to the chaplain, at least initially, as a transferential projection, a 'phantasy' (Laplanche and Pontalis 1973) of their unconscious imagination.

In this case, the chaplain who described himself as a 'rather formal looking, religious gentleman' (CHP001.42) was speaking intuitively about the transferential projection that his presence evoked in the dying woman he visited. In his particular case, he regarded her projection of her religious phantasies on to him as positive and helpful, if not therapeutic; but equally, he did recognise that the religious phantasies he evoked could at times be less helpful, if not actually negative:

very often … when I first meet somebody they will be … cagey towards me … even if they've asked to see me. (CHP001.42)

Without using the language of transference and countertransference, several chaplains in the research group described their experience of being the objects of another person's transferential projection of religious phantasies. Analysing their comments, I have identified four distinct ways in which positive and negative transferences can operate in the relationship between a chaplain and a dying person to effect different outcomes (Table 2.1). (It is worth noting here that I am defining 'positive' outcomes as those that facilitate some form of effective relationship, what counsellors and psychotherapists call a 'working alliance'; I am defining 'negative' outcomes as those that in someway undermine any such alliance.)

Table 2.1 Matrix of religious phantasies

Religious phantasies	'Positive' outcome	'Negative' outcome
Positive projection	**Strong form** 'Could you come back and see Mum? She was so pleased that you, just stopped to say hello' CHP001.05	**Ambivalent form** 'Oh lovely to see you, Vicar! (This is a representative of God; I must behave towards them in a certain way)' CHP103.04
Negative projection	**Mild form** 'Talk to me if you want to, but I'm not really that bothered' [the 'I'm-not-religious' response] CHP004.07	**Strong form** 'Bugger off, I don't want to talk to you!' CHP004.07

Positive projection: 'Positive' outcome

Describing an elderly woman as 'delighted to see me' (CHP001.02), one chaplain encapsulated the experience of many when they encounter a positive transference, in which the person's feelings appear to be favourable to the chaplain and seem to key in to positive memories of church and possibly childhood (Jacobs 1999, p.16). Significantly, the positive transference appears to result in a 'connection', which chaplains reported as somehow helpful:

And as she remembered this stuff ... she was just lightening, she was, you know, it was all becoming not quite so bad, somehow. And so, it was as if I took her to another place in that conversation, that in her recollection of her girlhood – which I think was basically happy – you know, she was taken then into quite a good space. (CHP001.02)

If positive transferences reconnect some people to securities associated with their 'residual faith', other people seem to find a degree of security in the positive phantasy that the chaplain is a fellow believer:

I do have to, I think, be secure in my own line; I think that's important too, that people have confidence that you are somebody who believes something. (CHP001.42)

Whether or not chaplains do believe the things that those they visit phantasise they believe, it seems that the benefit a sick person derives comes as much from the phantasy of their relationship to the chaplain as the actual content of the beliefs that the chaplain holds:

Sometimes patients feel such a sense of hopelessness that they want to be able to lean on somebody who has hope and somebody who has faith. I recently read an article in which someone was speaking about how someone had met the chaplain and had been journeying with them, and they said that the chaplain didn't seem to know much about what heaven would be like, 'But he gave me the assurance that where I was going was going to be okay, and that was good enough for me.' So in a sense they were leaning on the chaplain's sense of hope and of joy too ... often the chaplain's role will be to, you know, to almost provide that solid foundation, that solid sense of that the confidence that somebody may have in being able to lean on somebody else's faith for a time when they're not feeling very faith-full. (CHP021.07)

> One patient said to me that things were difficult and she
> was finding it hard to believe. But she said, 'I know that
> you believe it and I'm holding on to that' (CHP017).

Positive projection: 'Negative' outcome

This much noted, however, positive projections do not necessarily
guarantee positive outcomes and the 'ups' and 'downs' of a Snakes
and Ladders board offer a simile for the fickled, ambiguous nature
of positive projections. Assuming positive projections predictably
yield positive outcomes, one chaplain described her experience as
follows:

> If I got a positive response from somebody finding that
> I was a chaplain … I felt a little bit like the Snakes and
> Ladders board, that I'd gone straight up a ladder to a
> certain point, that I didn't have to work my way to get
> there … but I know where that person is at. (CHP012.10)

However, working with this simile, another chaplain expressed his
uncertainty about the positive nature of positive projections:

> When I meet a positive response I think I probably
> go *down* the snake … because their projections can be
> just as false as the negative projections that we have,
> and therefore you've still got stuff to work through.
> (CHP013.12)

Commenting later, in a one-to-one interview, he explained that
positive projections can be problematic because religiously minded
people often put the chaplain on a pedestal, with the result that
they may not 'necessarily reveal to you their real feelings and their
real thoughts about God' (CHP103.04):

> On the surface you can have a, kind of, niceness – 'Oh
> lovely to see you, Vicar!' 'How nice to see you … da-
> de-da-de-da.' But when you start to talk you get a sense
> that there's something boiling under the surface here
> that, you know, you could actually help to sort of, bring
> out, because another kind of transference that you get,
> might get from religious people is, 'This is a religious

person; this is a representative of God, representative of the Church, therefore I have to behave towards them in a certain way.' (CHP103.04)

Rosetta was a good example of the way in which religiously minded people can guard their otherwise positive projections. I had got to know Rosetta over many months in Day Care; occasionally I would sit with her and hold her hands and she would tell me about her (somewhat unorthodox) beliefs. She would bring books of daily readings for me to look at; at times she would talk proudly about her family and at times she would reveal the darker side of family life. Rosetta was a regular at the reflective prayer service.

Rosetta: 'You wouldn't want him here!'

I'd been sitting with Rosetta for some little while. We had spoken about her favourite food – curried goat (or perhaps chicken) and rice and peas. She had told me that she was still alive, thank God, and she said that Michael, her spiritual healer was away, but that Andrew was now coming regularly to give her healing.

'He can come in to see you in the hospice if he wants.'

She looked at me as if I'd said something rude.

'You wouldn't want him here!'

'Why not?'

Her eyes, dark and deep and full of years, questioned me.

We had come to the point where I needed to leave for today. I anticipated she would want me to pray with her, so I offered and she accepted. As she closed her eyes her leathery dark skin blushed with effortless calm; the many lines etching her features documented her path to grace. Rosetta didn't move into or 'switch on' to spirit, she was there already. I lent forward, elbows on knees, and took her hand. We touched across our separateness – me with my psychospiritualised, metaphorical hermeneutic, she with her innocent, open-handed stateliness.

'Loving God, thank you for all your love to us. Be with Rosetta, and her family; hold them in your love, surround them with your peace. Keep them safe.'

My prayer was simple and it was finished. But I was happy to sit quietly for a moment and allow God to do whatever God would do. We sat, my eyes closed. I opened them and looked at Rosetta, her eyes were closed. I sensed something was happening for her, so I sat. I stroked her hand, holding it with my left, running my right along her fingers. Her eyes remained closed. I watched her. She sat in dignified stillness; simply being. I began to feel my back stiffen. Rosetta was quietly indulging herself in whatever it was that she was experiencing. I began to feel my elbows stabbing the tops of my knees. Rosetta seemed aware only of her own awareness. I said 'Amen'. Rosetta stirred a little, but did not surface. I continued to stroke; to watch; to stiffen; to stab. Rosetta continued only in her state of serenity. I did that loud sighing thing that chaplains sometimes do to indicate 'time's up'! Rosetta was too far in to pay me heed. I stroked, watched, stiffened and stabbed some more.

Eventually, Rosetta emerged and smiled. She held me in her aged eyes.

'You didn't tell me you did healing as well!'

Negative projection: 'Negative' outcome

The chaplains in my research group recorded that, while negative transferential projections may manifest in extreme responses such as 'Bugger off, I don't want to talk to you!' (CHP004.07), far more common were the less extreme responses that, superficially at least, were more apathy than antipathy:

> an attitude that says (or it may not be said in words), 'Okay, talk to me if you want to, but I'm not really that bothered.' (CHP004.07)

Whether extreme or mild, chaplains experienced the negative transferential projections as 'hard work' (CHP012.10) or as 'a little barrier' to be overcome in order for the relationship to be therapeutic (CHP001.42). One very experienced chaplain described his experience of being the object of negative projections as 'very uncomfortable' and spoke candidly about the reluctance he feels when he has to meet a new person:

> I've been doing this for ten years, but I always hate – to a certain extent fear – that first encounter with a new person. (CHP004.07)

This very experienced spiritual carer's admission, that when he goes to meet a person for the first time he is to some extent afraid, may seem a little over-stated. However, encounters with people like the woman visiting in Room 20 are far from unique, and the experience of rejection is an acute possibility, real and present, in every new introduction. The point is that, while the rejection may be the rejection of a 'professional', or even a projection, in so far as what is being rejected is the perceived archetype – 'the Vicar' – it can be very difficult for any professional, to separate their 'personal-self' from their 'professional-self'. This is particularly the case for chaplains who, unlike other healthcare colleagues, only have themselves to offer to those for whom they care. Overall, the chaplains in my research group regarded strong negative transference, almost by definition, as unproductive of any positive outcome.

Negative projection: 'Positive' outcome

There are, of course, examples in which rejection has been turned into a positive working alliance: one chaplain reported that, having been told to 'Push off!' his 'innocuous' parting enquiry effected a positive response from an initially strong negative transferential projection (CHP103.03).

> There have been a number of instances where somebody has not wanted to see a chaplain … and that message hasn't got to me before I've gone in there, [laughs] and you know … To take an example, there was a guy … I went into his room, he said, 'Don't want anything to do with you, thank you!' Tried to explain that I wasn't going to push religion on him, I was just … interested in him as a person….
>
> 'No thank you. Don't want any of your stuff. Go on, push off!'
>
> So, I said, 'Okay,' I said … 'I will not come into your room again unless I hear from one of the other professionals that you'd like to see me.'
>
> 'That's right, and I shan't be asking for you …' Okay, so … on the doorstep as I was going I said, 'You been ill a long time?' or something like that, and, I asked him a totally innocuous question, and he then proceeded to tell me his, the whole history of his illness and the bit

about his life story; and he talked for about a half an hour solidly.

At the end of it I smiled and said to him, 'For somebody who didn't want to talk to a chaplain you've actually told me quite a lot.'

He goes, 'Oh, yeah. You can come and see me anytime.' (CHP103.03)

Several chaplains regarded any transferential projection of religious phantasy as a negative transference and resisted being anybody's transferential object. These chaplains took an obvious pleasure in being regarded by other healthcarers and those for whom they cared as not being religious:

> [I overheard] one of our nurses say to a family of a recently admitted patient, 'Would you like to see … a chaplain?' 'Oh, we're not religious.' And I heard the nurse say, 'Oh don't worry, our chaplain's not religious either.' And I thought, 'Yes!' because when I first started the nurses were, 'Oh, you want to talk about God, don't you!' (CHP003.11)

> They'll talk amongst themselves in the Day Hospice, you know, 'Oh, it's alright, you can go down to the chapel for a service because it's not like church and' – you know – 'she's not a normal vicar.' (CHP005.12)

Whatever might unconsciously motivate this resistance, one chaplain explained, cogently, that it had therapeutic purpose:

> I think as a chaplain you work with that transference by actually taking it on but at the same time disproving it, if that makes sense, by, kind of, breaking the barrier. (CHP004.04)

Although he was aware of misrepresenting the idea of transference, and went on to speak later about 'breaking the transference' (CHP004.07), he nonetheless understood the importance of acknowledging the phenomenon and working with (or against) it in the relationship with a person who is dying.

How chaplains work with negative transference

Counsellors and psychotherapists will want, at some point, to interpret the transference. Chaplains, however, work in a different way with transferential projections. Interpretation is not part of a chaplain's training or expectation, so the challenge, as they expressed it, is to find a way of overcoming the barriers presented by a person's negative projections. For this reason, one spoke of 'stay[ing] with' (CHP103.04) the negative; accepting it, receiving it:

> I don't mean acceptance in the sense that you willingly accept it, in the sense that you accept that this is what you're like to that person; but you receive it … you don't run away from it. So, one response was, 'Oh no, this person doesn't want anything to do with me because I'm religious.' So you withdraw from the situation, you retreat … then you only engage with the people who are already sympathetic towards what they see you as chaplain. Whereas, if you can stay with that – better word than receive it – stay with it (and I guess that's what I meant by 'break it' before), you're, kind of, working in the opposite direction to it, and it might result in confusion – 'This is, this is not how vicars are supposed to be!' – that it creates an opportunity for movement I think. (CHP103.04)

It is in the 'stay[ing] with' that the negative transference can come to be used positively to effect a 'shift in their idea of God' (CHP004.04), which – taking 'God' to represent the person's ultimate external 'locus of evaluation' (Rogers 2004, p.119) – might be described as therapeutic. His point becomes the more obvious in relation to the chaplain's role in staying with, or *receiving* the anger a person may express towards God:

> People are angry at God because of what's happened to them, so they're angry at you. (CHP103.04)

Such displaced anger at the chaplain, because she is perceived as in some way representing God, is perhaps just the clearest example of how a negative transferential projection can operate in practice. And it is the chaplain's natural, intuitive resistance towards being regarded as the object of another person's transferential projections that gives a key to how chaplains work with negative transference.

Central, among the chaplains in my research group, was the idea of 'being me' – the idea that I am not 'the [archetypal] Vicar'; I am my own, particular, individual person, with my own, particular individuality. Of course, it may be that their desire to be seen as 'me' was motivated by the same kind of unconscious fear of personal rejection that can trouble the first encounter with a new person. However, these chaplains seemed to adopt 'being me' as a position from which, or in which, to deconstruct what they considered to be wrong-headed and unhelpful preconceptions about God, specifically any emphasis on the judgemental nature of God.

> By meeting a religious figure, a perceived religious figure who is different and acts in a way that is different from how they would expect a religious figure to act and behave in terms of attitude and so on – and particularly in terms of acceptance – that may help people to move on in a particular direction. (CHP004.05)

This chaplain put particular emphasis on deconstructing the logic of the phantasy of religious judgement:

> the chaplain represents God,
> God is judgemental,
>   therefore the chaplain will be judgemental.

The implication is that by 'being me', in other words, by resisting being reduced to an archetype – 'the Vicar' – by demonstrating that she is her own individual personality, the chaplain deconstructs the other person's wrong-headed, unhelpful preconceptions of a judgemental God:

> the chaplain represents God,
> the chaplain is *not* judgemental,
>   therefore God might not (after all) be judgemental.

But also, the experience of being unconditionally accepted by the figure perceived to be religious may actually 'help people to move on in a particular direction' and, while the chaplain might not 'prescribe what that direction should be' (CHP004.05), it is likely to include the sense that the person is accepted as, and for who they are:

> the chaplain represents God,
> the chaplain accepts me as I am,
> > therefore God might (after all) accept me as I am.

As the 'rather formal looking, religious gentleman' put it:

> We got round to talking about her church, about ... when she'd been to Sunday School and her up-bringing and her faith, such as it was. She told me that she had been confirmed and had been to communion, but only as a girl, and she now thought that she couldn't have communion. So I said, obviously, that was not right and that if she did want to have communion that she was very welcome and that I would do that with her. She was thrilled, you know, and it was just, it was just astonishing, it was as if I'd offered her ... something really amazing, which for me was perfectly ordinary but for her was clearly something very special. (CHP001.05)

The point is that it is the contrast, even perhaps the contradiction, between the way a terminally-ill person expects the chaplain to be – in other words, as one who conforms to the preconceived archetype – and the way the chaplain is in herself – a particular individual who contradicts the archetype – that the person's relationship to the chaplain starts to become therapeutic:

> If the religious figure is a representative of God, and it's a God who is somebody you can't talk to, is somebody who's so far above contradiction, or so condemnatory, or so cold and distant, then you can, kind of, work against that negative transference, and that in itself can be a positive thing. (CHP103.01)

For this chaplain, this deconstruction of the archetype is the thing that 'can be creative about the role of chaplain' (CHP004.04); for him, the moment of the 'I'm-not-religious response' is the point 'where most of the creativity happens' (CHP004.07), because:

that's the point at which you can work through to a meaningful relationship, in which the person's spiritual issues can emerge. (CHP004.08)

The following is a good example of how by, 'staying with' and 'being me', it is possible for a chaplain to deconstruct the logic of a negative projection:

[She] told me straight out that she'd explored all religions and she didn't believe in any of them and she had no intention of talking to me about them and if that's what I wanted I could go away. And I said, 'No, that's fine, we don't have to talk about that.'

So I knew her for about six months; never, ever talked anything about religion or faith with her. She told her daughter, unbeknown to me, that she wanted me to take her funeral service, but she had told her family way back that she wanted a humanist funeral service. So when she died we talked with the family, who were Christians, about how we were going to do something that honoured her views but could be right for them. And the family concluded that … we could pray for the family, but she wouldn't want prayers for herself; that was the way that we did it.

So at the beginning of the service I explained what was what and why we were doing it this way, and at the end of the service as people were going out, I had this sense that I'd actually failed her; that here was this lady, she had died, and she and I hadn't talked about these things at all.

And an elderly lady came over to me and she said, 'I'm So-and-so, I'm her best friend but I live [a distance away] and we've just had telephone contact.' And she said, 'Last week she 'phoned me up. "D'you know," she said, "that chaplain at the hospice, she's made me think that maybe there is a God after all".' And I thought, 'Well I've said nothing and done nothing, but …' So I just hope that by being me and I suppose demonstrating that love and acceptance that it just might make those who have no faith at least begin to think. (CHP003.11)

Summary

All human contact evokes a transferential response, positive or negative; relationships with healthcare professionals have a particular transferential loading and the phantasies a person projects onto the chaplain are likely to have a religious if not archetypal character (Hinksman 1999, p.101; Watts *et al.* 2002, pp.262–3). If a person requests a chaplain visit, the chaplain can expect to encounter positive transferential phantasies. In this case, the person requesting the visit is likely to be 'delighted' (CHP001.02): they may feel secure in being with someone they believe shares their beliefs and understands the needs they feel able to express; or they may feel reconnected with associations from what is left of their 'residual faith'. These are positive outcomes from positive transferential projections. However, not all relationships, with those who are 'delighted' to see them, result in a positive outcome. Some religiously minded people may idealise the chaplain so that they are unable either to feel safe or to be reconnected and consequently they will be unable to disclose 'their real feelings and their real thoughts about God' (CHP103.04).

While chaplains can expect to be the object of positive transference where a person requests their visit, they can be less confident when they 'cold-call' or when they respond to referral made by another professional – the healthcarer may have coaxed them into seeing the chaplain; or the person may be unaware that a referral has been made. Some people will be delighted by the visit, but the chaplain is just as likely to encounter apathy or antipathy as the object of the person's negative transferential projection. Strong negative transferences seem always to be unproductive of any positive outcome, whereas even being told to 'Push off!' (CHP103.03) may, with a little gentle persistence, lead to an outcome in which the person feels valued and accepted. Key to a positive outcome is the chaplain's ability to use their own presence to deconstruct the logic of the judgemental religious phantasy – the chaplain represents God; God is judgemental; therefore the chaplain will be judgemental. Chaplains do this when they stay-*with* the negative transference, accepting or receiving the negative projection and at the same time resisting it. By being themselves, 'being me' and so contradicting the person's expectation of what the chaplain will be – particularly when the person is directing their anger towards the one they see as God's representative – the chaplain can demonstrate a preparedness to be in human contact with a suffering person *no-matter-what*, and at this point their relationship can become creatively therapeutic.

Chapter 3

Accompanying Presence

Karl: They want us to let go

'Have you met Karl yet?'

No, I hadn't, so the specialist registrar, gave me some background.

'Youngish-man, mid-50s. He's been a high-flyer in marketing. His wife, Ingrid, is in publishing. But the thing is, she won't let go. She's wanting second opinions and she's taking him off for appointments with radiographers and goodness knows what. The social worker was with him yesterday, and spoke about how it can be hard sometimes to talk to those who are close about things, and that she was there if he needed to "sound off" to someone. Next thing, Ingrid is having a go at the social worker saying we're going behind her back telling Karl when he gets fed up of talking to her, he can talk to us. Really, Ingrid needs to be "on board" that he's not getting any better and it's just not helping him to be going off for more treatments.'

A nurse caught me in the corridor and expressed her concerns that Ingrid was 'in denial'.

My social work colleague confirmed her difficult conversation, but her take was more about the angst being generated around the couple by staff.

'The staff seem to want them to be in a place of accepting; but they're not there yet.'

I recalled Stephen Levine's words: 'To attempt to steal "denial" from another is an act of righteousness and separatism' (1986, p.163).

Perhaps understandably, I was apprehensive about visiting Karl, but I determined I should cross the threshold into his room.

As I approached, there was a curious warning note on the door: Harvey is visiting, please take care not to let him escape!

Harvey, it turned out, was an exquisitely featured oriental cat, who paraded his captivating feline chic as if the room was literally his catwalk.

Karl welcomed me and we talked about Harvey. Karl had been brought up with cats, and Ingrid had recently bought Harvey as a present to keep Karl company. I fished around for possible points of contact between us. I discovered he liked sport and we talked about football; he wore a T-shirt that pictured a galaxy and we got on to astronomy. Karl told me about his 'high-powered' job: 'I was the sort of person you would get the vacuum cleaner out for!' As I left, Karl said I should, 'Come again.'

Over the next couple of weeks, I got to know more about Karl's eclectic interest in sport, about his passion for cats, about his love of the universe, and about his career in marketing. When I meet Ingrid, I was cautious. She was the 'angst-ridden' one, the driver for more treatment, the one 'in denial', the one who might have a go at me. I trod carefully.

As it was, Ingrid welcomed me with warmth and the offer of red wine ('Thanks, but not at work!'). She told me about their life together in Europe and the Far East. She spoke about Harvey and other pets that at various times had been part of Karl's life. She offered me some Dutch honey cake and the remains of some raspberries, and she told me about the wine she and Karl had drunk last evening. I listened, and Ingrid spoke. She seemed charged with an energetic vitality. We didn't speak about Karl's illness, and I left wondering what I had been there for.

'Have you seen Karl today?'

No I hadn't. So the specialist registrar gave me some background.

'He's been to see about radiotherapy, but the professor said there's no point in further treatment. He's not well enough. When I was with him, Karl seemed to accept this, but then Ingrid wants to try something else.'

When I met Karl and Ingrid, Ingrid expressed frustration about what had happened. It was beginning to look to me like 'poor Karl' was being dragged about in a futile pursuit of ... what? Then Ingrid showed her hand:

'I can't just sit back and do nothing, and just watch what happens. I need to do something. Better to do something than nothing, than just accept what comes.'

'You feel like you'd be letting Karl down if you didn't.'

'Yes!'

'Is that what you want Karl? Do you want to keep trying?'

He nodded. I was unsure whether this was for his sake or Ingrid's; but either way, he was decided.

Days later, I saw Ingrid sitting in the coffee lounge and asked if I could join her. The nurses were changing Karl, Harvey was with him, and Ingrid was taking a bit of time to work on a magazine article.

'It's crazy here. I'm not criticising anyone, they all do a wonderful job here. But it's just ... they're really good at what they do, but they want us to let go. It's all about making him comfortable and keeping him pain free. They can't cope with me wanting to do something more. They need us to comply. I'd rather do anything rather than nothing. I'd rather Karl died in the ambulance on the way rather than just let go. They say he can't keep having steroids; they're not good for him. And I say, if it gives him a bit more quality of life for a few days more ... what's the alternative? We know what will happen when they stop. He'll get worse, and that'll be the end.'

The nurse tending Karl approached looking concerned: 'Ingrid!' Her voice was professional, but it betrayed her controlled disquiet. 'While we were cleaning Karl, he got a bit distressed.' I began to fear the worst. 'Harvey must have sensed this ... and he disappeared under the bed ... and ... he found your hold-all bag and ... I'm afraid he "went to the toilet" ... in the bag!'

Ingrid was not in denial. She was as realistic as anyone I have ever met. She knew exactly what she was doing, and she knew why she was doing what she was doing. She loved Karl, and to let him go without a fight would be the utmost betrayal. And if that meant standing up to doctors, consultants, even professors, then up she would stand.

Through Ingrid I saw the extent to which palliative healthcarers need people to be 'on board', to be where we need them to be, to share our agenda so that we can feel able and supported to work with them. Palliative healthcarers don't have the luxury of ignoring death; it's our work-a-day reality. If we ignore it, if we imagine it only as the possibility of a remote future, we would fail those in our care. It is, then, an immeasurable help when those we are caring for, or at least their close carers are 'on board'. But Ingrid's determination to be faithful, to not betray the man who for 40 years had been her best friend, questioned the cause of the distress healthcarers experience around people who are dying or their close carers who 'Do not go gentle into that good night', but who instead 'rage against the dying of the light'.

Karl and Ingrid were not ready to be in any place their palliative healthcare professionals may have felt they should be. But they were in the place where they needed to be to get on with their work, which on balance seemed the more important.

Like many other chaplains, but unlike most other healthcare professionals, I do not conceptualise my work in terms of a clinical agenda or a therapeutic aim. In general, healthcare chaplains seem not to see themselves as being there to *do* any particular thing with or for the people with whom they work, instead they speak of being with them in a way that is genuinely what Rogers terms 'person centred' (1980):

> Take a simple example, I mean, there might be an issue about, let's say, very, very common situation in a hospice where somebody's gonna be discharged to a nursing home and doesn't wanna go, okay. Now maybe, it could be that every other professional is there to actually try and make going into a nursing home much more acceptable for that person, okay. Now I, as a chaplain, wouldn't be attempting to do that – I might sometimes be enlisted to do that by other professionals, 'Would you go and have a talk with them (Name)?' Right? But nevertheless, what I'm there for is to hear how awful it feels for that patient to be going into a nursing home. (CHP103.05)

This chaplain's 'simple example' can be read as a practical exposition of what Heidegger (1962) terms 'dwelling' (*Aufenthalt*). Taking a word that, when used reflexively, carries the ideas of 'to stay at a place' and 'to hold back or refrain' (p.89, n.2), Heidegger uses it to define a way of 'Being-in-the-world' that is concerned with 'holding-oneself-back from any manipulation or utilization' (p.89) in order to perceive 'the present-at-hand' (p.89). Expounding Heidegger, Ladkin (2006) comments that 'dwelling' demands particular attention is paid to the *being* of the other, such that the one attending should 'suspend their sense of self' (p.93). According to Ladkin, 'Heidegger refers to this as "presencing", and he suggests that through such presencing, the "Being of Beings" comes into manifestation' (p.93).

As such, 'dwelling', 'holding-oneself-back from any manipulation or utilization' (Heidegger 1962, p.89), has a strong resonance with what Lines (2006) terms spiritually-centred counselling, which he describes as:

> a particular mode of interaction that calls practitioners to step aside from their preferred manner of working to engage in a therapeutic process of *being with being,* and to respond to their clients in a reciprocal engagement as though both are on a continuing journey of transcending.
> (Lines 2006, p.2, emphasis added)

Put in these terms, dwelling with an other has an inherently spiritual quality, that resonates with what Buber (1958) describes as the *I–Thou* relationship, in which 'the *Thou* becomes present' (p.26), and which in Buddhist therapy is compassion [*karuna*] that 'sees through the eyes of the other … without any private agenda' (Brazier 1995, p.195).

Chaplains appear intuitively to have understood and incorporated this spiritual quality into their work with dying people, for example, in the way they make use of their own being in their being-*with* a dying other. One chaplain explained how her experiences in caring for her dying husband and of living with her own cancer informed her being-*with*. For her, 'just being' was sometimes purely instinctual:

> Sometimes feel I don't know what I'm doing and I don't know what I can do. All I can do is go and, and be there.
> (CHP003.19)

Physical presence: Being-*there*

Whatever else dwelling means, it is predicated on the physical presence: to dwell with a person who is suffering, a healthcarer has to be in the same physical space as they are. This involves witnessing the suffering, but more importantly, it means putting oneself in a position where it is not possible to look away, which would be an implicit rejection.

Chaplains understand the importance of being physically present: one chaplain accounted for his being-*with* very much in terms of his physical presence demonstrated through his physical contact. Expounding on his sense of what might have been going on between him and a person who was dying, whose hand he had been holding, he reflected:

> I wanted to tell him that I was there, and I hope for him, you know, it's that sense that, 'I know you. You're coming to the end of life, your life, and some people struggle with death and dying, but, I'll hold your hand; I'll be there for you'. (CHP002.14)

Physical contact with a dying hand instinctively and immediately communicates physical presence. However, this chaplain understood that other layers of communication were carried by his physical presence: a sense of the dying person's continued physical connectedness to their community, which implied a psychological-emotional connectedness:

> that sense that, even though he was away from the place where I'd normally see him at home, and he was in a hospital setting, you'd still taken that time to come out and see him. (CHP002.16)

The layers of communication carried by physical presence were expressed by one chaplain who saw her physical presence as primarily communicating 'you're not alone':

> I think the 'me getting in there' is just being, is sitting with them in this place that is hard and difficult, not necessarily doing anything, just simply sitting there so that they're not in there on their own. (CHP003.14)

But she also recognised the emotional import that her physical presence carried:

> I think when you're alone in a frightening place it's overwhelming. There's a hymn ... one of the verses talks about 'I will hold the Christ light for you, in the darkness

of your fear,' and I think that's what our role is; perhaps it's just to be there and hold the light. (CHP003.15)

For this reason, she summarised her job as 'just being whatever it is that they need me to be' (CHP003.02).

Thomas: Separate lives

The soundtrack to my nursing home meeting with Thomas came from a too-loud radio sounding from the next room and the discords of a noisy corridor. Thomas seemed unbothered by the edge-of-awareness intrusions, but I found the 'golden oldies' radio station impossible to ignore – it was playing the tunes from my youth and I tried to punctuate our silences with conversation.

> *Foot-tapping to the driving beat of Elton John's 'Saturday Night's Alright for Fighting', I was halfway through the chorus before I caught myself singing another familiar song!*

'Have you had a good week?'

> *A trolley rattled along the corridor and a resident's bell added counterpoint to the cacophony!*

'Not bad. I've had quite a lot of pain. I've not been outside.' Thomas's African accent was clipped, his speech deliberate and measured. He sat on his bed, only a twisted sheet protecting his modesty; his hand gestures were as deliberated as his words; his wasted legs naked and motionless.

> *A plaintive voice called from a neighbouring room!*

I watched Thomas and wondered about his childhood in the forests of Africa. I enquired about his years before coming to England, but he revealed little. He looked a long way from home, lost in this peace-less place, full of noise and busy-ness.

> *Freddie Mercury's unmistakable voice announced 'Bohemian Rhapsody' with well-timed questions about whether this life is real or just a fantasy!*

Thomas had been referred to me because his clinical nurse specialist felt I might be able to offer him some support; but how, in any meaningful way, could I touch his life?

What seemed to me an insensitively (but probably hard-of-hearingly) loud knock on the door announced what seemed to me an indiscreetly (but probably rushed-off-the-feetly) quick opening and the arrival of an evening meal delivered by what appeared to me to be an indifferently (but probably lacking-in-trainingly) harried male Filipino care assistant. With the practised familiarity of daily routine, the Filipino carer cleared and wiped Thomas's table then arranged the meal tray with all the dignified respect due to a TV dinner. I wondered if he had affected his pleasant manner because I was in the room.

From 1985, Phil Collins' song 'Separate Lives' elbowed
its way into my awareness!

And I found myself a spectator to the scene: three men alone together in some anonymous bedroom, in some anonymous nursing home; strangers and foreigners, our journeys begun at different times, from different corners of the wide world – from Africa, the Philippines, the North of England; struggling to communicate in a language we shared, labouring with accents that were heavy and unfamiliar. I wondered what circumstances had conspired to bring us all together to this place, and in what meaningful ways our lives were touching each other at this time: synchronised isolation, moving about each other in contiguous proximity. Or was there some other level of meeting?

The Filipino carer left us alone.

'Looks tasty.' I was sure I didn't believe what I said, but I wanted (or rather needed) to try to make some contact.

'I think it's kidney pie.'

'Is it okay?'

Thomas pushed out his bottom lip. 'Okay.'

He wanted a cold drink, but the water in his jug was tepid. I offered to get some fresh and took the jug. When I returned, Thomas had rung his bell and the Filipino carer had returned. He took away the jug I had just refilled, emptied it, refilled it and returned it once again to Thomas's table. I watched the farce unfold. It was as if I had tried to reach into Thomas's world, but he couldn't or wouldn't notice my presence.

So I offered to read his book to him. And he seemed genuinely grateful.

'Thank you so much. That was very kind of you.'

'I'll come and see you again.'

'Thank you so much. That would be very kind of you.'

Emotional presence: Being-*with*

As my encounter with Thomas illustrates, dwelling is predicated on the physical presence, but being-*with* is more than physical proximity. Despite Heidegger's assertion that dwelling lets 'beings be as the beings which they are' (Heidegger 1993, p.125), Levinas (1951) asserts that 'The other is a being and counts as such' (p.5), and it is in addressing the other 'face to face' (*le face à face*, p.9) that we understand the other. Entering the physical space of a person they are seeking to offer care, the chaplain encounters the face of the dying other and, because 'the primary experience of being is situated at the level of emotion' (Levinas 1957, p.41), she enters their emotional space.

As one chaplain observed, being in the emotional space of a person who is without hope, facing their face 'in its mortality' with its 'summons', its 'demands', its 'claims' (Levinas 1989, p.125) can 'grind staff down' (CHP003.19), leaving them unsure of what they have to offer. But as one chaplain commented:

> That's maybe where we come in, at least we're still saying, 'Well I'm still gonna come and listen to you.' But I often think in those situations, 'I don't know what I should be doing here.' And I think, if nothing else, it is just the physical presence and the holding the hand and the listening to what's being said. (CHP003.19)

This chaplain expressed intuitively what Levinas (1999) expressed philosophically:

> *The Human* consists precisely in opening oneself to the death of the other, in being preoccupied with his or her death ... it is no longer just a question of going toward the other when he is dying, but of answering *with one's presence* to the mortality of the living. (Cited in Cohen 2006, p.26, emphasis added)

In other words, the extent to which they respond to the call to be open to what Levinas (1969) calls the 'impossibility of possibility' (cited in Cohen 2006, p.30), is the extent to which any member of the palliative care staff may already have all that they need to offer spiritual care. However, in my experience, not all healthcarers, including palliative healthcarers, have the capacity to be open to the 'impossibility of possibility'. Those who are able to be open, will be able to stay with a person who is living their 'impossibility of possibility' without trying to change a situation that cannot be changed; those who lack the capacity to be open in this way, will probably try in some way to 'make things better', either for the person who is dying or for themselves.

I want to argue that, while healthcarers may be able to offer first-class physical care, not all healthcarers are able to offer spiritual care. In part, this is to do with where we get our sense of identity and fulfilment; but equally, it is to do with the difficulties we have in facing our death anxiety (which I will return to in Chapter 6). My argument with those, like McSherry (2001; 2006), who claim it is the responsibility of healthcarers in general and nurses in particular to deliver spiritual care, is that it is unethical to demand that all nurses and healthcarers should undertake the psychospiritual work that is necessary to equip them to face their personal anxieties about their own death. In my view, those who offer first-class physical care are able to *contribute* to the spiritual care of sick and dying people precisely because they are offering first-class physical care, which they can enhance by learning care skills associated with showing respect and treating with dignity (Saunders 1988).

Joan: So many questions

'I don't believe in some old gentleman up in the sky with a long white beard.'

'Neither do I.'

There was little unusual about a Christian minister denying that the out of date iconography immortalised in Renaissance art had little to do with modern conceptions of God, but my reply seemed to disarm Joan and her eyes softened.

I'd been told that she was troubled by lots of questions about dying, about meeting her maker, about what might come next; and she wasted no time in getting down to business.

So, lying in her bed, she began to speak about her doubts, her attempts at faith and her lack of belief, and her concerns about judgement. And as I sat and watched and listened I remembered what I'd been taught by another person I'd visited: that sometimes people use the language of religion and belief as a way of speaking about themselves, a way of describing their inner, emotional landscape. In Joan's case, the landscape of her interior was breaking apart, in-step with the breaking apart of her physical world. It seemed to me that her words about wanting to believe, about wanting to have something to hold on to but yet not being able to believe, were her way of speaking about a need for certainty. Not necessarily, now, a certainty about God or the afterlife – she wasn't inviting me to persuade her about the truths of the ancient Creed. Joan knew she was dying, and 'there was nothing to be done about it,' and against this reality she seemed to be looking for something that could hold her firm against the collapse of all things, although it wasn't clear what that anchor might be.

'I'm not really a believer. I suppose I think that I want to live on in others and what they think about me. But there's only my husband – we didn't have any children – and I don't really have many friends left.'

She looked away. She slipped her hand out from underneath the sheet and placed it near mine. I put my hand on hers and she began stroking me. She looked back.

'People like you ... forgive me ... people like you, you do a lot of good; but you don't always let people come forward.'

'I don't think I understand what you mean.' But I didn't get an answer ... not one I understood.

'I'm going to be whipped for every sin I ever committed. I don't think I want that ... I often revert to levity ... So many questions, there's always been so many questions. For years I tried to find answers.'

I don't know where the idea came from, but I found myself thinking: 'There's usually only one.' I wondered if I should speak my thought – it was an interpretation and it might not be the right time. But then how much time did she have left in which the 'right time' was going to offer itself? She'd begged forgiveness from me for being direct; maybe, with her forgiveness, I could be direct with her.

'There's usually only one.'

'What do you mean?'

'Well, there's so many questions, but there's usually only one main question that troubles us. It sounds to me ... forgive me ... it sounds to me as if you're looking for certainty ... that you matter.'

Again she looked away, her eyes reddened and became full. I wondered if I'd been too direct too soon. I held the silence.

'Yes!' she whispered.

'You do matter.' It was reassurance, and reassurance doesn't work, but I needed to say it.

She looked back.

'I think dying is very safe. I think that, whether you believe in God or whether you believe in nature, I think we go back to where we came from, I think we're welcomed back into the place that we came from.' She looked away, her reddened eyes still full.

'Will you come and see me again?'

Holding hands with Joan, we faced together her 'impossibility of possibility'. Whether or not I had said the right words at the right time, she seemed to be glad to have someone to hold her hand in the darkness.

One chaplain described her work in terms of entering a dying person's darkness in order to 'hold' something of their experience:

> I think to enter it is to be able to hold whatever it is, and for them to see that you're not disturbed by it; that nothing that they can be or say would affect the relationship that you're building, I think that's very key for chaplains, the way that we are present to the other. (CHP005.03)

The idea that chaplains 'hold' and are 'not disturbed by' what a dying person is experiencing resonates with a set of ideas developed by the British psychoanalyst Winnicott (1954a; 1954b). Winnicott argued that the analyst's ability to *hold* a person in analysis and to *survive* the hatred directed at them because of their failures as an analyst could effect what he termed 'a regression' (1954b, p.261). In Winnicott's theory, 'regression' is 'a highly organized ego-defence mechanism', 'a normal phenomenon that can properly be studied in the healthy person' (1954a, p.281). For Winnicott, normal, healthy individuals will defend the self against what he terms 'environmental failure' by a '*freezing of the failure situation*' while maintaining the unconscious assumption that an 'opportunity will occur at a later date for a renewed experience in which the failure situation will be able to be unfrozen and re-experienced' (p.281). His clinical point is that, if '*the analyst can hold the patient*' (1954b, p.261), he or she may facilitate the 'regression to dependence' (p.255) that will be 'the opportunity for correction of inadequate adaptation-to-need in the past history of the patient, that is to say, in the patient's infancy management' (p.261).

Chaplains obviously do not engage in the kind of analytic work Winnicott undertook. Nonetheless, it seems that, perhaps intuitively, they have understood the importance of holding and have incorporated something of this ability to hold into the core of their practice. Chaplains understand that this kind of holding of a person, whether that person is themselves dying or whether they are someone living with a dying person, eases their sense of isolation and can help to dissipate some of their anxiety.

Arthur: Staying with the bewildered

Arthur's face perfectly expressed his experience of the moment. 'I'm bewildered,' he said, but the weary stoop, the slow, aimless shuffle, the little-boy-lost stance had already spoken for him.

He was quick to fill me in on the background to our meeting: his wife's apparently sudden illness; the misdiagnosis that potentially had squandered valuable treatment time; her rapid decline and admission to the hospice; and her lapse into her final silent sleep.

She coughed. Arthur moved quickly to her side, pressing his head close to her face. 'Irene? Irene! IRENE!' She breathed; he breathed. He explained that she had done this several times. His relief was as palpable as his anxiety.

As his relative composure returned, Arthur began to speak about his faith interests. He had wanted a spiritual healer to visit his wife, and had contacted a healing organisation. But his experience disappointed him.

'I hadn't realised she was foreign until she said her name. But she couldn't understand what I told her. I got a letter next day and she'd got Irene's name wrong: Hannah! How do you get to Hannah from Irene ... I don't know.' A healer had visited, but the visit coincided with Arthur's return home to feed the cat, and he missed it.

'She came in and stood by Irene for about 15 minutes, then left.'

'What was it you were hoping for from the healer?'

'Well, they say they help you to feel better. I think I'm looking for a miracle.'

Arthur spoke about healers in days gone by.

'Where are they now? You can't get hold of them. They've all got answer phones with messages that say they can be contacted between 7 and 9 in the evening. That's not what I call a healer. They've all got jobs, but I'd have thought that a healer would have spent most of his life in prayer to God to help him in his work.'

Arthur spoke about his life together with Irene. He told me about their meeting when they were in the armed forces and about their move to the Home Counties where they set up home. He said that they had little money and so had holidayed in England and explored the countryside. He said that they didn't join groups, churches or otherwise, but that they had had some involvement with a Bible study group. Arthur described a couple who had kept themselves to themselves. They had no children. They had no friends.

One person who had influenced Arthur, a man whom he had followed for many years, was Herbert W. Armstrong of the *Plain Truth* magazine. Arthur seemed almost wistful as he spoke about Armstrong's prophecies of crises that would hit the world, in particular the calamity predicted to befall in 1975. Yet the calamities hadn't come, and Arthur seemed somehow disappointed.

'I don't take the magazine now. It's become a general church magazine that says all religions are the same. Someone wrote to the editor about the predictions, and he said that Armstrong was wrong!'

Arthur reflected on the changing world and reminded me that 'The Bible tells us there will be a falling away.'

'Britain has opened the floodgates to immigrants,' he told me, and he confided his difficulty in understanding the foreign doctor who had spoken to him in the hospice about his wife's deterioration. 'I could hardly understand a word he said. Fancy having a doctor who can't even ...' Then, realising he was speaking to the man's colleague, he cut himself short.

I began to wonder why he was talking to me like this. Why was he telling me this stuff? There we were, alone in a room together with his dying wife, with whom he had done 'everything together' and without whom he said he could not imagine a future, and here he was talking to a stranger about a world peopled with strangers who were hostile to all that might make him secure; all he valued and held to be good. Why, I wondered, was he telling me this, now?

In my mind, I recapped his monologues of disappointment, his stories of expectations disenchanted by doctors who failed to diagnose, healers who failed to work miracles, spiritual guides who failed to deliver judgement. And I began to wonder about his early years' experience.

'Do you have family nearby?'

Arthur had had two brothers and one sister, but they had all died; one of cancer: '... the youngest was ten years older than me. I didn't see much of my dad. He got a job north of the river. He left at six in the morning and got home at seven. He had his dinner and read the paper. When I was little, he was gone before I got up, and I was in bed when he came home.'

And I imagined a young boy growing up in a world of strong, independent but distant others; a young boy without a role model, alienated from the adult world of his siblings, a boy unable to live and move comfortably in the social world of adults, unable to make and keep friends; a boy who found solace and succour in the care of a doting female, but whose loving dyad was under constant threat by the return of the patriarchal absence; a boy who became a draughtsman, who designed and drew micro-environments over which he had total control; a boy easily disappointed by others, disappointed that prophecies of damnation failed to materialise.

So I began to form the view that, in describing his fears about the outer 'real' world, as he saw it, he was actually telling me something about his inner spiritual world, as he experienced it. Where it had once been a world in which he had found a supportive confederate in his now dying wife, Arthur's world was fast becoming a dark, foreboding landscape in which he was increasingly feeling isolated, estranged and alone. Arthur knew he was about to become truly alone in a world he found frightening and his experience of existential lostness was intensified with every laboured breath Irene took.

The question for me, as his hospice-provided spiritual guide, was how to walk with him for that part of his journey that we were sharing together.

In the first instance, I attempted to nurse his disenchantment with healers and spiritual guides. I offered to pray with Irene and, knowing Arthur was listening, I held her hand and spoke gently to her about the love of God. But I knew that, like others, I was failing to give him what he felt he really needed, because what he really needed was a miracle.

After that, I spent as much time as I could with Arthur: visiting him in Irene's room; walking with him to the coffee lounge; accepting his self-acknowledged idiosyncrasies; and trying, feebly, to enter his crumbling world, albeit for the briefest of spans.

Irene died while I was on duty, and I was glad to be able to find Arthur before he left the hospice. He told me he had been with her as she died and that, to his surprise, he had felt relief. But I wondered if Arthur's spiritual distress was somehow related to losing his mother ... all over again.

In a way that is congruent with Rogers' (2004) observation that the process of therapy enables a person to gain 'awareness of [their own] experience', what he terms 'the experiencing of experience' (p.76), being physically present and emotionally available, the chaplain is in a place to experience something of the experience of the dying person. By experiencing a measure of that experience, chaplains may give the dying person permission to experience their own experience (Nolan 2008b).

In a very similar way, the chaplain's physical presence and emotional availability situates her in a place where it is possible for her to experience something of the other person's experience, and in so doing to give that person permission to experience their own experience:

> There are times when I look at patients who are feeling hopeless and I suppose I feel hopeless with them and for them, but at least I'm allowing them to feel hopeless, whereas other people maybe aren't. And I think when you just leave somebody feeling, 'If you won't let me talk about it, then what I'm feeling must be so awful that I can't share it with anybody else and I'm left here with it on my own.' Whereas, if we let people talk about it, then it loses some of its awfulness, I think. (CHP003.21)

Summary

Once the chaplain has accepted and worked with the other person's transferential projection – positively, by offering a sense of security or reconnection, or negatively, by deconstructing the projection – the chaplain can become an accompanier, one who can and will stay-*with*. As an accompanier, chaplains have no therapeutic aim or professional agenda with those for whom they care; they are not accompanying in order to do something *to* or *for* the other so much as simply to be someone *with* them.

In this way, chaplains intuitively understand the concept of dwelling or being-*with* another. Dwelling implies active engagement with another, but without any well-meant intention to manipulate them; it means accompanying the person, being-*with* them in a way that allows that person to be the being they are rather than the being that the chaplain, or anyone else, may wish or need them to be. Such accompanying extends to accepting the person's right to die the death they need to die ('on their feet' if necessary; or with quiet acceptance; or with raging 'against the dying of the light'), rather than the 'good death' prescribed by palliative care.

As an accompanier, the chaplain attends to the soul (*psyché*) of the person (West 2004, p.144), *face à face* (Levinas 1951, p.9) in a way that treats the other as a *Thou* not an *It* (Buber 1958). And in being physically present (being-*there*) and emotionally available (being-*with*), the chaplain not only experiences something of the dying person's experience, but contains and, crucially, survives the experience in a way that allows the person to experience their own experience as contained.

Chapter 4

Comforting Presence

Phoebe: A very tired 86-year-old

Chaplain:	Hello Phoebe! How are you?
Phoebe:	Not very well.
Chaplain:	It's not going too well.
Phoebe:	I've had enough.
Chaplain:	You're tired.
Phoebe:	Very tired.
Chaplain:	Have you been poorly for a long time?
Phoebe:	(*Nods*) For two months.
Chaplain:	And you've had enough.
Phoebe:	(*Nods*)
Pause	
Chaplain:	I understand you have two daughters.
Phoebe:	Two in this country and one in South Africa. One of them is going back to South Africa shortly. But the older one is staying in London.
Chaplain:	(*Hearing a slight accent*) Are you from South Africa?
Phoebe:	No. Two of my daughters married and settled there.
Chaplain:	Have you been out there.
Phoebe:	I used to go every year.
Pause	
Chaplain:	Has faith been important to you Phoebe?
Phoebe:	From time to time.
Chaplain:	Is this one of those times?
Phoebe:	(*Nods*)
Chaplain:	Would you like me to say a prayer for you?
Phoebe:	That would be nice.
Chaplain:	What would you like me to pray for?

Phoebe: It would have to be me leaving this world.
Chaplain: Shall I pray for your daughters as well?
Phoebe: I think they'll be alright.
Chaplain: Loving God, Thank you for your love,
            and thank you for your love to Phoebe
            down through the years.
            I ask that you will be with her now
            as she is ready to come back to you.
            Give her peace and courage,
            and hold her in your arms. Amen.
Chaplain: God bless you, Phoebe.
Phoebe: Thank you. That was very nice.

The rather basic idea that chaplains comfort people who are dying was something I unwittingly ignored in the initial round of interviews with individual chaplains. On reflection, this was probably because I bear a prejudice against the term – it seems too close to all those media parodies of vicars dispensing 'comfort' in the form of 'tea and sympathy'. As one of my research group acknowledged:

> I suddenly, sort of, think fluffy cushions and, you know, therefore, I'm a bit cautious about what do we mean by comfort? (CHP102.12)

Despite my researcher's blind spot to the term, the self-perception of chaplains as 'bringers-of-comfort' had actually been present in the initial interviews:

> I obviously tried to comfort her and to explain to her that it was all going to be alright. (CHP001.20)

> They were in the middle of a real problem … but they felt as though they wanted some support and comfort at that particular time and so they turned to the chaplain. (CHP002.27)

> Starting from the baseline that I cannot give people hope, but I can be with people without any kind of hope in a way that is helpful and comforting and, perhaps, strengthening for them. (CHP005.08)

In fact, this last chaplain drew attention to the Latin etymology of the concept, 'to strengthen' (*confortare*).

Challenged to make explicit the uncritical assumptions of one more taken-for-granted concept – 'if we're talking about comfort we'll have to define what we mean by "comfort"' (CHP013.12) – chaplains did speak about physical comfort:

> We do want to make people comfortable physically and, you know, sometimes that, you know, means a clean, fresh pillowcase. (CHP102.12)

Such physical comfort is self-evidently important in healthcare (Johnson 2007, p.455), but the more pervasive idea among chaplains was that of bringing 'spiritual comfort'.

One chaplain described the content of being comfortable as, to 'Feel at ease with; to be peaceful about; to be accepting of' (CHP101.12). He speculated that some people might find comfort in the presence of the chaplain:

> In the same way as you are comforted by the fact that a doctor or nurse is present, therefore you think, 'That's good, they will give me a pill, or they will do something that is going to make me feel better.' So there is something about their professionalism, maybe, that is comforting – I think you could draw the analogy there ... I think sometimes just presence does give reassurance and comfort. (CHP101.12)

This view was echoed by his colleague:

> I think being present, that thing, just being with them ... they're not alone, if they don't want to be. Allowing them to express their despair and all of that, which I think does sometimes release the pressure, which then allows them to relax a bit, and that can make them more comfortable. (CHP102.13)

Chaplains seem to make their 'comforting presence' available both actively, in friendship building, and (apparently) passively, by being a silent presence.

Active presence

Speaking about meeting people 'where they are', one chaplain spoke of working with two young men, both of whom were agnostic: one who 'all he wanted was a friend, somebody who was going to be there for him, not take him anywhere he didn't want to be' (CHP101.10); the other:

> was into fast cars and he liked a pint, and that's what we did: we went out in our fast cars, we'd go down to the pub and have a pint, and we'd talk. And sometimes the conversation would come round to, you know, his TVR and how many miles per gallon it didn't do. There would be practical bits about how he was trying to set his wife, his family and the financial bits up. Then we'd just have a laugh. But when he was dying, and he died at home, I was one of the last people he called; and I went to see him and we'd talk, and we didn't talk anything about God, we didn't do a prayer, I didn't give him a blessing, he just wanted something of my presence, and for me that was enough as well, and it was clearly enough for him. (CHP101.10)

By definition, building a friendship means building a relationship of trust in which sometimes urgent questions can be addressed. One chaplain noted how, once a person has been given a terminal diagnosis, they may:

> begin to have questions; questions they've never really thought about before. And they're not necessarily religious questions, they're existential questions: Why am I here? What's the real purpose of my life? (CHP101.04)

Interestingly, this chaplain did not see his role to be that of supplying orthodox theological answers. For him, answers that bring comfort to existential questions are answers that have their own existential authenticity:

> The only authentic answer for them will be their own answer, the one they come to themselves. So my job is to help them form their own answer, the one that will actually comfort them and give them a sense of peace

as they face the end of their journey, or earthly journey anyway. (CHP101.04)

As an example, he reported a conversation he had had in a particular service user group:

> I posed that question to them once, I said, 'Most people think that when we die somehow life goes on.' And one of the big roughy-toughies, with all the tattoos on him said, 'Well I don't', he said, 'I think when you're dead, you're bloody dead mate!' And then there was a pause … And then he said something quite beautiful, he said, 'And I believe somehow I live on in my children.' (CHP101.05)

In every case, a person's authentic answers only emerge when they feel safe enough to say what they really think. This sense of safety is only possible between people who trust each other, and creating a sense of safety is core to what chaplains do:

> I think people like to feel that they will be safe somehow. That's what we do, I think, here in this place and that's what I ask God to do, to 'hold people safe'. (CHP102.03)

To 'hold people safe' is a good way to describe palliative care: hospices 'hold safe' people who are extremely vulnerable. Michael's vulnerability was related to his brain tumour and its unpredictable effects on him. Nonetheless, we were able to build a relationship and as his condition deteriorated over time, we continued to meet. At times, I found our conversations confusing, but it seemed important to continue to be with Michael as he struggled with his unanswerable questions.

Michael: 'Because'!

'If you had a decision, what would you do with the rest of your life if you had 20 minutes to live?'

I had just stood up to leave; I'd said my usual, 'It's been good to meet with you. Can I come and see you again?' I'd put away the chair I'd been sitting on, and crossed the room towards the door. It was just at that point that Michael posed his question, and although it had the ring of philosophical abstraction about it, I heard it as existentially authentic.

Michael had been in the hospice for several months. He had come from hospital after a close brush with death. He had not been expected to survive, but had recovered and, when I met him, he spoke openly about having time he had not expected to have. Not that he spoke very coherently. His brain tumour had left him thinking and talking in loops. He would begin speaking about something then, as if a phrase had got caught in his mind, he would repeat the same thing like a sampled refrain through his conversation.

I liked Michael; everyone liked Michael. He had about him an honest openness, an almost child-like innocence. He told me about the break-up of his marriage and how, with the help of his men's group, he had worked to make a friend of his ex-wife so that his children would continue to have the support of two parents. Part of the way in which he had come to terms with this episode was to say, quite frequently, 'You make a mess, we all do, but you admit it, you pick yourself up and do your best.' It felt important for our relationship for me to share with Michael that I had had a similar experience of divorce and recovery.

Over the weeks of his stay, Michael deteriorated. He fitted and became physically more frail. His 'loops' became more pronounced, but he retained his endearing openness.

On the day he posed his question we'd been speaking about his need to make a decision. As I pulled up a chair, Michael told me, 'I've been thinking about something I have to decide about ... about what to do, where I go from here. I'm not sure what I should be doing, where I should be going ... I have to think about what I'm going to do with the rest of my life.'

His decision seemed redundant. Michael's prognosis wasn't exactly short, but nor was it that long. Yet it seemed important to give Michael time so, with little expectation, I sat and listened and Michael struggled with his question.

'It's a decision I've got to think about, what I should be doing, where I should be going ... I have to think about what I'm going to do with the rest of my life ... and it's a political decision ... it's the kind of decision about what to do and it has political ... you know.'

Michael became animated. He looked about, as if to check we were not being overheard.

'I'll tell you, because I can ... I'm 45 and I have a decision to make ... and it's sort of political ... and it's about what I'm going to do ... with the rest of my life. It's a decision that is kind of political, it has political ... if you went into the Cabinet Office ...'

And so he continued. Michael digressed on to telling me about his involvement in politics, so I took it that he was trying to process something from his past experience, something that was somehow connecting with what he was experiencing here in the present. But I had no idea what, so I just sat with him. Eventually, it was time for me to leave, and as I moved towards the door Michael posed his question: 'What would you do with the rest of your life if you had 20 minutes to live?'

Something seemed to be speaking through the wandering disorder of Michael's thoughts.

'I suppose I'd want to spend it with the people who loved me.'

'Why?'

Wow – wrong reply – this was not what Michael was supposed to say, and I was not ready for his response!

I echoed to buy a little time to think.

'Why? ... Because I'd feel safe with them.'

'Why?'

Another wrong reply; but it seemed genuine. It was as though Michael was trying to work out some reason for being around; some reason to be in the short time, the '20 minutes' he might have left to him.

'Why? ... Because being with them would make me feel ... not so much special as ... valued; worthwhile.'

'Why? Why are you worthwhile?'

Once upon a time, back in the days when my world was simple and uncomplicated, I would have hesitated only for a breath before replying, 'Because God loves you and showed that in sending Jesus.' But my world is no longer so straightforward and the religious simplicities no longer satisfy as they used to. I needed to find something to say to Michael that made sense to me and that might make some sense to him.

So I told him: 'You're worthwhile because you're a human being; because you are alive; because you make a difference to those you love. You make them feel good.'

Did that make sense? On one level, it was the same kind of answer my mother used to give me when I posed her an awkward question: 'Because!' And if I pushed her a bit harder: 'Because I said so!'

Michael seemed to be asking: 'Why am I worthwhile?' And I wondered which answer fits best?

'Because God loves you'?

'Because you are'?

'Because'!

Then I added, '... you make them feel good because you give to them.' But this was more than I wanted to say. I'd introduced a qualification about being as doing, when all I had really wanted to say was: 'Michael, you're worthwhile because you are.'

'... or because you take? Maybe you take more than you give.'

'Maybe you do. Or maybe you're given more.'

'I'll need to think about that. Maybe it's political.'

Passive presence

The chaplain's 'comforting presence' may also be communicated passively; simply by staying silently in the pain of the other person's present experience. One chaplain recorded his sense of bemusement that his silence could speak eloquently and with such effect:

> I've been into rooms and, you know, I might have been a little bit uncomfortable about where we are in that moment with somebody's last bits of their life. And you may be struggling for words or what to say, and quite often I say nothing, and then I'm very surprised when they say to me the next day ... 'And what you said was such a comfort.' And I think back, and I think, 'Actually, I don't think I said anything' – in fact I can remember feeling 'I'm uncomfortable myself.' But staying in that uncomfy place with them is what we're called to do, and I think staying with them gives them presence and does give them comfort. (CHP101.13)

Another chaplain spoke with some passion about a former colleague's ability to be a 'comforting presence' by silently sitting with a dying person:

> He just sat with people, and would sit for an hour and a half if somebody needed him to, just holding their hands ... too often the nursing staff still say, 'Oh, don't need to go to him; he's dying.' And we say, 'No, well we

will go and just sit and be with him; maybe he may not appear conscious, but I want to be with that person and accompany them, whether they appear to be aware of us or not.' (CHP102.05)

It is not clear why this kind of accompanying seems strengthening to people who are dying. Unable to rationalise, this chaplain was nevertheless convinced that it was an important factor in why some people die peacefully and gracefully. It may be that an unconscious person derives comfort from 'the soothing voice' (CHP102.14).

Alfred: The 'Ya-neva-know' defence

I'd been asked to see Alfred. He was agitated again, 'spiritually distressed'.

He was pleased to see me and, in his usual, courteous, charming way, he invited me to 'Please, come and sit down sir', and to talk with him. But within minutes, Alfred's eyes began to glaze and grow heavy, his voice softened and his head nodded and fell low on to his chest.

I decided I could sit a while with him, moving might wake him and there seemed an easy peace between us. I began to meditate and just 'be-*with*' Alfred.

And as I sat, my awareness expanded in the present; outside, the blackbirds sang their way into the room a counterpoint to the voices of visitors as they ambled between coffee lounge and ailing relative; inside, the breeze wafted thoughtfully in through the room taking the edge from the muggier than usual late summer afternoon; and beyond, the invasive glances of people passing the open door intruded into what was becoming our room. Alfred was peaceful, his sleep deepened.

And, unnoticed, my mind slipped away over my day, expanding my awareness into the very near past. I remembered Kelly and her question about how she should plan her soon to be late husband's funeral. She spoke about what for me seemed an interesting problem: 'Not sharing one faith, it's difficult to know what to do for the best; for everyone.' I had agreed that it had all been so straightforward back in the days 'when we were all C-of-E', then we'd just turn up at the church and the vicar would read his prayers, and everyone would know what to expect, and everyone was happy (or as happy as the circumstances would accommodate); and I reflected to myself that now we have to be more grown up, take more of our own responsibility and make more of our own decisions.

Still unnoticed, my unruly mind continued expanding my awareness and I recalled the mid-day chaplains' meeting I'd attended and the unspoken, barely acknowledged anxiety provoked by a *Times* article highlighting chaplaincy and questioning the difference between chaplains and 'psychologists or therapists', and asking what it is that distinguishes chaplains from other related professions.

When I realised where I'd wandered, I returned my awareness back to the room and back to Alfred – still watching him sleep, content in his oblivion – and I wondered how long I could, should, would stay. He was in a deep sleep now, cheeks inflating, deflating, in rhythmic content. Should I stay? Was this good use of my time? Perhaps I should go. I made a move to leave and then changed my mind. I felt somehow comfortable in a way that I projected I would feel uncomfortable if I left.

So I stayed, not lingering but intending. And staying in the present and the near past, Alfred's sleep, Kelly's difficulty, the chaplains' anxiety, merged into a singular train of thought:

> ... maybe being with this sleeping man was somehow helping him ...
>
> ... maybe what's good about 'now' (now that we don't all share one faith) as opposed to 'then' (when we were all C-of-E) is that we now have the freedom to respond creatively to death, dying and grief; we can construct the kinds of funeral service that are special, particular to the person we grieve ...
>
> ... maybe what distinguishes chaplains from psychologists or therapists is that, when chaplains manage to get it 'right' it is because we allow ourselves to respond to the individual in ways that are 'inspired' (breathed, spirited), ways that permit the kind of independent and creative freedom that comes primarily from being in a place of spiritual maturity that is itself the result of a continual working with and on and through our own 'stuff', our own way of being – that comes from living the examined life ...
>
> ... maybe being with this sleeping man was somehow helping him because it was a response to him that went

> beyond the obvious – he's asleep now, so it's time to
> go – and instead worked with the realisation that it was
> the presence of another that comforted him to sleep ...

Again I was aware that I was wondering how long I should stay with Alfred, and that this was an indication of my own discomfort about what I was doing; an indication of how driven I am by the imperative to do and to be seen (by the passing eyes that invaded our room) to be doing rather than living with my conviction that what matters is my ability to be a being-*with*: Was my being with him while he slept a good use of my time? Ought I to be somewhere else ... with someone else ... someone who wasn't asleep ... someone who would more obviously, more visibly, less embarrassingly, benefit from my presence?

'But', I reasoned with myself, 'maybe my staying was helpful to him. He had been agitated, now he was calm; he had been childishly regressive, now he was sleeping like a baby.'

And I began to think that sitting with a sleeping man might just be an example of that very 'inspired' independent, creative response which I was able to make because I was comfortable with my self.

Or perhaps I was just playing the fool to my own self-deception? Was I making use of the much beloved 'Ya-never-know' defence – 'Maybe I'm helping him, maybe I'm not. But then, "Ya-never-know".'

The nice thing about the 'Ya-never-know' defence is that 'Ya just never know'; but the trouble with the 'Ya-never-know' defence is that 'Ya-*will*-never-know' ...

> ... although Alfred had previously told me that he liked
> me being with him ...
> ... and he had previously said that I had just the right
> calming effect on him ...
> ... so, 'Ya-never-know'.

Another chaplain offered a more mystical, theological explanation of the effect of his presence:

> Maybe there is something of my own journey that holds
> me and is capable of holding them as well. Ultimately,
> maybe, that's a bit of God. Maybe I am a bit of God,
> maybe that'd be a way of looking at it, and maybe that
> is – I was going to say visible – but, er, tangible, in a way.
> (CHP101.15)

For him, 'comforting presence' seemed to communicate to the dying person a sense that they are loved:

> There was something I said to a lady not so long ago, who was a very … one of these ladies who had to be doing something – 'I've got to do something!' So she came to me, and she said, 'I want to plan his funeral!', and, sort of, got a pencil and paper out there. And I said, 'No, I think there's plenty of time for that. What I'd like you to do is actually spend more time with him.' Clearly, that was an uncomfy place for her, but that's where he, that's what he wanted; he just wanted her presence. She found that difficult … I mean, for her, being a doing person, it would have more meaning and be more worthwhile planning the next bit; to, kind of, bring her back to a point where she would understand that in doing nothing but just being, just holding his hand, just speaking to him even though he couldn't respond was worthwhile. (CHP101.19)

Whether or not this chaplain was mystically 'a bit of God' with the person for whom he was caring, his experience resonates with the mysticism of Buber's (1958) higher-level *I–Thou* relationship, where the *I*, retaining awareness of the particulars of the *It*, connects with the universal in the *Thou* to undo at least something of 'The melancholy of our fate' (p.39).

Writing in 1923, between world wars that divided the 20th century, Buber (1958) brings a particular perspective to the conditions of our human relating. A Viennese, Jewish mystic, existentialist, Buber characterises human relationships in terms of *I–Thou* and *I–It*. At first glance, Buber's simple division seems direct, almost self-evident, immediately understandable and applicable: in the *I–Thou* relationship, Buber seems to be affirming a way of relating, that is, person-to-person (subject–subject), mutual and reciprocal, and contrasting this with the *I–It* relationship, which turns the other into a mere object (subject–object). This is the way some psychotherapists interpret Buber. For example, Clarkson (2003) describes the person-to-person relationship as a relationship 'characterised by the *here-and-now existential encounter* between two people. It involves mutual participation in the process and recognition that each is changed by the other. Its field is not object relations, but *subject relations*' (p.17).

However, Buber's division is more mystical and profound than it first appears. For Buber, awareness of our self as an individual self comes as we acquire language and learn to speak. Before that point, our awareness of the other is indistinct, unformed, pre-conscious, primordial; amodal. We may have a sense of '*I-affecting-Thou* and *Thou-affecting-I*' (Buber 1958, p.37), but we lack any real sense of who that *I* or *Thou* actually are. Significantly, in this state, without any real sense of self, we perceive no separation between our self and the environment which we inhabit. In this state, the relation of *I* to *Thou* is direct, immediate and mutual.

It is as we acquire language, and begin naming the *Thou*'s that populate our world, that we start to become aware that we are separate from and other to those *Thou*'s that we are naming as 'things' (objects). Then the pre-conscious union of '*I-affecting-Thou* and *Thou-affecting-I*' fractures, the *I* splitting off to emerge as 'a single element' (p.37), conscious and separate, and conscious of being separate. This is the world in which we must all live and survive; this is the everyday world of *I–It*, in which, by continuous 'peering observation' and analysis, the separate *I* inevitably and necessarily isolates 'particulars and objectifies them ... without any feeling of universality' (p.46).

Buber (1958) describes this separation as 'The melancholy of our fate' (p.39), inevitable and necessary, in which the *Thou* has become forgotten. Yet it is not beyond remembering, because 'True beings are lived in the *present*' (p.26, emphasis added). For Buber, the present is not a point in time so much as the moment of meeting when one person is present to another: 'the real, filled present, exists only in so far as actual presentness, meeting, and relation exist. The present arises only in virtue of the fact that the *Thou* becomes present' (p.26). In other words, the present *is* the possibility of a way of being in which is 'our life with spiritual beings, where the relation, being without speech, yet begins' (p.130). His point is that the *I–Thou* relationship can be returned in the *present*, in such a way that *I* connects with the universal in *Thou* and, at the same time, is aware of and retains understanding about the particulars of *It*. In short, the *I–Thou* relationship is one that understands and works with the contradiction of the human condition, the double bind of separation and connection. A healthcarer who is able to work in the *I–Thou* relationship would be able to operate in the paradox that they are an *I* separate from and, at the same time, connected to a *Thou*.

Rogers (2004) understood something of Buber's philosophico-theological insight when he writes that the 'essence of some of the deepest parts of therapy seems to be a unity of experiencing' (p.202) in which the person and the therapist experience their feelings 'without any conscious thought about it' (p.202). Such quality of comforting presence implies what Rogers describes as an 'atmosphere which simply demonstrates "I care"; not "I care for you *if* you behave thus and so"' (p.283), which is love in all but name.

Several chaplains spoke of being-*with* a dying other explicitly in terms of loving that person:

> My job is to enable people to feel loved and valued and accepted just as they are, by me – and hopefully by other staff; by God, if they're open to hearing that … but it's to let them know that just as they are is okay. (CHP003.07)

> They need to know that they are unconditionally loved, and that nothing that they've done can affect – or not done – can affect their relationship with God. (CHP005.14)

> When you're feeling unlovely you can feel unloved, and maybe part of our job is to restore love. And if God is Love, then we bring something of that to that situation, and again that might be tangible but inexplicable, unexplainable. (CHP101.17)

Almost by way of counterpoint, one chaplain wanted to qualify the quality of the love that he offers, describing it as a 'professional being with', a being-*with* that is 'professionally circumscribed' (CHP103.06). He made his point with reference to a book on pastoral theology (Campbell 1984):

> …called *Moderated Love*, which I think is a lovely phrase really, is that while you're there in that setting it may feel

like love, but actually it's not the kind of love that you have – I was going to say in real life as though this is not real, I don't mean that – in your non-professional life, in your personal life; the kind of love which is reciprocal, which you live by as well as the person that you love living by. This is something that I am doing in this situation. (CHP103.06)

He developed this, describing how his being-*with* would be very different should his own child be terminally-ill:

This is something that I'm doing as a professional, I'm not gonna take it out with me, or I may take it to supervision, I may take it to another professional to talk about, but, you know what I mean? …this is not gonna be burdening me once I leave that room. (CHP103.06)

He has a point, of course, and to a degree Campbell (1984) himself agrees: 'the professional does not and cannot love (or hate) a person as a relative or friend does. There is a necessary detachment in professional care' (p.85), and Campbell contrasts the 'hardheadedness' and 'consistency in the care offered' by professionals with the 'more erratic and turbulent attempts to help which emanate from family and friends' (p.85). Nonetheless, Campbell insists that the 'moderated love' offered by professionals '*is* love':

It is a reaching out to another in the desire to enhance the value which is seen, and such reaching-out requires the non-rational connection which feeling alone can create. (Campbell 1984, p.85)

Writing personally about professional love, Cassidy (1988), a hospice medical director, observes that healthcare professionals, 'trained to *suppress* our love', keep a safe distance from people who are dying with the result that they meet as 'professional and client, not as the frail human beings that we all are' (p.22). In her experience, 'those facing death have a particularly urgent need of human warmth and honest straightforward communication' (p.26). She goes on graphically to describe simply holding (physically) this person, stripped of all her intervention skills, medical and counselling, left simply as a being-*with* (pp.61–64).

Clearly, there is a delicate balance to be maintained between professionalism, on the one hand, and humanity, on the other. People who are seriously ill and/or dying need all the professional skills that are available to them; but they also need all the humanity that those who have the skills can bring to their profession. As Dame Cicely Saunders put it:

> If we can come together not only in our professional capacity but also in our common, vulnerable humanity, there may be no need of words on our part, only of respect and concerned listening. (Saunders 2005, p.xx)

Sally: Chipping away at a big block of terror

Several times I'd been to see the young man in Room 12, and several times I'd been frustrated because ... now the cleaners were cleaning ... now the nurses were attending ... now he was in the bathroom ... But I'd already introduced myself to the young woman in the room next door; she was free, so I knocked and said hello.

'Pull up a chair, do, I'm just going through some papers that my husband brought in, it's just to keep my mind active, I find that I start to wander off after a while; I've been here for ... what is it ... over a week now and ... well ... we had a difficult time over the weekend, I finally found a way to tell my son; I was given a prognosis on Friday, and I've been told that I should think in terms of months – of course, they don't have crystal balls – so I managed to find a way to ... he's got to get used to the idea of not just having a mum who's long-term sick ... I don't want him to come home from school one day and be told ... I think it's better that he can get used to the idea; I've begun to notice the changes in myself, that I'm not so well ... I don't hear so well out of this [left] ear and this [left] side is much weaker ... I can still get up and shuffle out to the loo, and I want to keep that going as long as I can; so I held his head in my lap for a moment, and it was hard ... he got upset ... I held him and it felt like that moment when he was first born, you know, when you hold a baby ... close ... and it was as if those 11 years just melted away [tears] ... and I remembered every single moment of those 11 years ... and ... what I'd give to be able to relive every one of those moments ... all over again ... they talk about a broken heart and it was heartbreaking, it was like a physical pain, I felt a pain in my chest.

'But he and his father are good – they're very good. He's started doing things with him that I love, like skiing; so they went off skiing together for the first time last year, and he loved it; and sailing, they go up to the Lake District, I think it's wonderful that they can look out the tent and see all that, all the things that I love – not me! Camping's not for me ... a nice, cosy B & B or pub-hotel ... that's more my cup of tea; but I told him that he'll always have me with him [tears] ... I said, "I'll always be at your shoulder."

'The counsellor has been very helpful, she suggested to him – because he's not wanted to come in to the hospice (I don't think he likes to see me in a hospital setting, he keeps on saying, "When are you coming home, Mummy? When are you coming home?") – she suggested that he could come in with his little dog, and as soon as she said that he wanted to come in right away; she's been very good ... she's spent time with both me and my husband ... and now it's time for my son.

'This has been a good time for me, it had been such a stressful time before I came in from our little holiday that was supposed to be good for us – it was a disaster – but I've had complementary therapy and people like you who listen and I've managed to unwind; mind you, while I've been here my husband's managed to break the washing machine and the boiler; but he's looked after, we've got some really good friends, he's got a very good group from the sports club – although they look rough and stubbly, they're really big softies – and there's a group of women who we know from school and when he comes home, there's often a pyrex dish of pasta or whatever, so he's got food ... they're very good like that, so I know he's looked after – he knows what I'm like ... if I'd been at home I'd be trying to mend things and do things, but I can't here, so I rest, I've just got to lie in bed and ... be.

'We've made wills ... nobody likes to think about that, but we've done that ... and if he dies before my son is 18 ... we have some absolutely wonderful friends – friends I would trust with my life ... with my life – who would take care of my son; and I've thought about my funeral – I've managed to face that one, so I've been chipping away at a big block of terror – bit by bit, I do this little bit, like the will, and I know that it's done ... and it is done, and I can forget about it, put it away ... literally in a drawer, and forget about it, then I can take the next little bit of the block and have a go at that.

'But I get tired … it sounds terrible, but I've had to monitor the visitors, the nurses have had to tell some people that I'm having a rest – there was one old friend that I'd forgotten was coming and I saw her, but she's great, she always has lots of stories, but she doesn't always know when enough is enough, I get a bit tired before they bring the lunch around.'

I took the hint (an uninvited guest who stayed too long): 'Are you getting a bit tired now?'

'I am actually, and they'll start bring lunch around in about 15 minutes.'

The challenge for healthcarers is to be *both* fully professional *and* fully human; the privilege for chaplains is that their professionalism demands their humanity, to the extent that they are able to relinquish their own protective masks.

Summary

As accompaniers, chaplains comfort the dying soul – not in the anodyne, 'tea and sympathy' sense of comfort, but in the original meaning of *confortare*.

Typically, the chaplain does this by building a trusting friendship in which existentially urgent questions can be asked and can be given honest, occasionally unorthodox, replies that enable a person to find their own authentic and personally satisfying answers. Equally typical will be the chaplain's preparedness to remain with the authenticity of the person's experience, often in a place beyond where words are effective.

Chaplains find it difficult to account for the comforting effect their presence has on those for whom they care: some offer mystical, theological explanations; others merely acknowledge it as a fact of their work. My own speculation is that a dying person's experience of anxiety and uncertainty trips a 'regression to dependence' (Winnicott 1954b, p.255) in which the comforting presence of an empathic other has the capacity to recapitulate something of their primordial *infans*, pre-linguistic experience of the *I–Thou* relationship, where they were comforted by an empathic (m)other. Regardless of how accurate such speculation may be, chaplains locate their ability to comfort those for whom they care in their capacity to love them with what they see is the love of God.

Chapter 5

Hopeful Presence

Yvonne: 'Cancer ... welcome aboard'!

I invited myself to join Yvonne as she sat quietly in the courtyard shade. We exchanged politenesses about her visitors and my weekend before moving on to her trips to Lourdes. Yvonne told me about her first reluctant trip, griping and grumbling because someone had paid for her to go, but she didn't want to be there. Snapping at the kindnesses of the 'kids' as she called them, the young volunteer helpers, Yvonne complained, 'And when they started singing *Ave Maria* when they saw the station ... if I could have opened a window and thrown myself out, I would have done!'

It wasn't until the middle of the week, when 'one of the kids' sat on her bed and explained to Yvonne that she'd paid for herself to come and help on this trip, that she'd given up her holiday and put herself out to be there, and that Yvonne 'should think herself lucky' and 'stop being so miserable', that things changed and Yvonne began to enjoy the experience. 'But by then I'd lost three days of the pilgrimage.'

As we spoke, she was planning her third visit.

'My faith is deeper now, much deeper; it's never been so strong. That's because it's simple. I used to read a lot about theology: the Bible and the books about theology; about why he said this and what he meant about that. But it's now much simpler. It's not about: he said this because ... and he said that because ... but what he really meant was ... It's about he's the boss and what he says is okay. He knows what's best and if he gives something to me, if he gives me a terminal-illness, it must be for the best. It's as simple as that. I just have to trust that he knows what's best for me.'

'It's about relationship.'

'Yeah.'

'What made the difference?'

'Reading *The Shack* helped. Have you read it?'

'I've started it.'

Yvonne gave me her synopsis of the plot. 'In there, the Holy Spirit is called "the Gather of Tears". As Catholics, we don't really understand the Trinity, do we? Now, when I feel like crying I remember the Holy Spirit as "the Gather of Tears", and I feel really close to it.'

Yvonne asked me what I had been doing and we got on to talking about my research with chaplains' experiences working with dying people and my interest in hope. I explained a little about my project.

'There is a lot of hope about, but it's not the sort of hope that you're thinking of. Like a lot of cancer patients, I hope that there will be a breakthrough, that they will find some new treatment. I hope that I will die in here and I hope that my friends will be around for me. I hope for these kinds of things. But that's not hope in the way that you're thinking.

'When I was first diagnosed, I didn't wail and get upset. I just said, "Okay, I've got cancer," and I got on with it. I soon realised … well, after a bit of time I came to realise, that the cancer was part of me and if I tried to fight it then I was fighting myself, and it wouldn't work. So I started to put into practice what we used to tell people when I was a CPN [Community Psychiatric Nurse]. When you get up in the morning and you're brushing your teeth, look in the mirror and say: "Good morning. You're not a bad person. Have a good day!" So I did that. I looked in the mirror and I said, "Good morning. You're not a bad person. And cancer … welcome aboard!"'

If I'm honest, what she said shocked me.

'I'm interested in the way you talk about not fighting yourself. I've met quite a few people with a terminal-illness who talk about hoping to do this or do that before they die. They're hanging on so that they might … I don't know … see their new grandchild perhaps, and they talk about *fighting* the cancer. But it sounds like you're talking about *accepting* your situation.'

'I'm really grateful to God that I've got cancer and that I haven't got Alzheimer's. When I worked as a CPN I saw what happened to people who get Alzheimer's. I've always used my brain and I couldn't stand the thought of losing that.'

'So what is hope to you, then?'

'I hope that I will be able to die in here. I hope that I will have done enough to go somewhere that's not hell. I hope that I won't become miserable so that my friends don't want to be around me. You know, you can really piss people off, if you'll pardon my French, by being a miserable old bag. No, I'm really grateful to God that I haven't got Alzheimer's. I'm happy. And I think it shows ... doesn't it?'

Chaplains may not think specifically in terms of helping dying people find hope, but they nonetheless regard hope as an important part of their work with dying people. This is because, when it comes to spiritual care, chaplains intuitively understand hope to be a significant contributor to a person's well-*being*. Yet, as Yvonne told me, it is 'not hope in the way that you're thinking', not hope in the way hope is conventionally constructed. In interviewing chaplains, I found that she was right and I was struck by the fact that *hope was not explicit in how chaplains described their experience of working with dying people.* As one chaplain put it:

> I think we do bring hope, but I don't feel that we necessarily set out to bring it, but that what we do can bring it and can give them light. (CHP012.07)

This contrasts strongly with the importance nurse researchers assume for hope (Garrard and Wrigley 2009; Reynolds 2008) and it suggests that chaplains see hope, and perhaps therefore spiritual distress, in a way that is very different to other healthcarers, who often regard the spiritual distress associated with loss of hope as pathological. I will have more to say on this in the next chapter, but for now, it is enough to note that writers as prominent as Saunders (1988) and McSherry (2006) conceive spiritual distress primarily in terms of pain that needs to be relieved.

Several of the chaplains I interviewed wanted to define hope in terms of what it might be in the *present*. One spoke of 'hope for the present' (CHP012.07), another of 'hope for today' (CHP012.01). As another explained:

> We're not necessarily involved with hope in the future, but somehow that actually the present can be liveable with, however bad it might seem ... hope that the

present is, not necessarily okay, but okay not to be okay,
perhaps – hope in the present. (CHP013.02)

Reconceptualising hope as 'hope in the present' runs counter to
common sense (Rousseau 2000, p.117) and also to those concept
analyses that regard hope as future oriented (Benzein and Saveman
1998, p.323; Chi 2007, p.415; Johnson 2007, p.454). As Garrard
and Wrigley (2009) put it, hope has an 'in-built orientation towards
the future' (p.38) and it seems self-evident that it is directed towards
the future realisation of an as yet unfulfilled desire: our hope *for* or
hope *that* is a desire towards something that, at least potentially, is
yet to be realised. Given that both theologians (Moltmann 1967;
Rumbold 1986; Herbert 2006) and healthcare professionals (Herth
1990; Nekolaichuk and Bruera 1998; MacLeod and Carter 1999;
Chi 2007; Garrard and Wrigley 2009), assume hope to be future
oriented, the idea of 'hope in the present', 'hope for the present' or
'hope for today' fundamentally redefines the concept.

Despite this common sense understanding, redefining hope
in terms of the present is congruent with the traditional use of
'hopefully', in the sense of to be 'in a hopeful manner' (*Compact
Oxford English Dictionary* 2003). As such, 'hope in the present' seems
to be observable in the lives of people like Yvonne and to be of a
different order from the kind of resigned and passive acceptance
others express.

Ray: 'Nuthin' I can do about it'

Ray: My aunt told me, 'You got lovely eyes and eyelashes. You'll kill the girls.'

Chaplain: And did you?

Ray: Naw! I wasn't bothered. I s'pose I shouldn't say this, but I preferred to go for a drink and mess about with cars. I think there's two types of love really: the physical and ... s'pose you could say the spiritual.

Chaplain: And yours was the second.

Ray: Yeah!

Chaplain: You had a good relationship?

Ray: Yeah! But it weren't based on sex. I think my wife was glad she found me. We had our moments ... there's times when you want to be a rampant old man. But I'd rather have a good dinner ... at least it lasts longer! I think of meself as in God's waiting room, now.

Chaplain: Does that worry you?

Ray: Naw! I just accept it.

Chaplain: What helps you accept it?

Ray: I just get on with things. Nuthin' I can do about it is there?

Living with a 'hopeful manner', what might be called 'hope in the present tense', carries the idea that hope can be or can become an attribute of being; as Smith-Stoner and Frost (1998) put it, hope is 'the energy to move forward' (p.48). Whether, in this case, hope fuels resilience or somehow becomes resilience is moot. The International Resilience Project defines resilience as 'a universal capacity which allows a person ... to prevent, minimise or overcome the damaging effects of adversity' (Monroe and Oliviere 2007, p.1). For their part, Herth (1990), Farran, Herth and Popovich (1995), Rousseau (2000), Felder (2004), Chi (2007), Johnson (2007) and Reynolds (2008) are among those who see hope as a resource for coping. Whatever is the case, it seems that, in the face of a terminal diagnosis, hope can be reconfigured: not simply that a dying person may adjust their specific or particularised *hopes* (Nekolaichuk and Bruera 1998, p.38), which in any case may be expected to change, since hope is intimately related to desire (Chi 2007, p.415; Garrard and Wrigley 2009, p.39) and desire is in constant evolution. But *hope* itself may become reconfigured: no longer as *hope for recovery*, but hope now as *hope beyond recovery*.

Reconfiguring hope: From hope to hopeful

A problem inherent with defining any concept is that a definition will invariably raise more questions than it can answer. The nursing literature has had a sustained interest in analysing concepts (Paley 1996; Rodgers 2000; Risjord 2009) and this desire to clarify has contributed to an overabundance of hope definitions. Benzein and Saveman (1998) identify 54 variants (p.323) and Cutcliffe (2004) records the impossibility of finding one definition that 'encapsulates all that hope is and specifically how it relates to health, disease and healthcare' (p.26). Despite such pessimism, philosophers Garrard and Wrigley (2009) feel able to describe what they term a 'standard account' of hope (p.39), which they see as based on a belief that an anticipated (and hence future) desire will be fulfilled. In the standard account:

> hope is analysed into a belief–desire pair: a person hopes for a state of affairs, P, if and only if she desires that P, and believes that it is possible, though not certain, that P will come about. (Garrard and Wrigley 2009, p.39)

For Garrard and Wrigley, this standard account underpins the ethical problem posed to healthcare professionals: whether, in order to maintain hope and its beneficent effect, healthcare professionals should deceive a dying person about the likely outcome of their illness; or whether, out of respect for individual autonomy, they should honestly inform the person, and so risk leaving them to despair.

The general approach to structuring the experience of hope is to regard it as 'a point along a single continuum ranging from hopefulness to hopelessness' (Nekolaichuk, Jevne and Maguire 1999, p.602). Typical of such simple, two-tier models of hope is that articulated by Farran *et al.* (1995), who propose three 'levels' to the structure of hope. For Farran *et al.*, hopelessness is the pathological level, an experience that marks people whose hope has been challenged by difficult life experiences such that they succumb to the challenge, or 'may even have given up' (p.26). At the level of what Farran *et al.* term 'pathological hope', hopelessness is characterised by 'diminished physical, mental, and spiritual functioning and quality of life' and in its most extreme forms this pathology may result in depression, mental illness, suicidal ideation or 'some other form of sociopathy' (p.26). At the intermediate level, 'challenged hope', Farran *et al.* suggest that hope and hopelessness are structured with similar characteristics, in so far as a person facing a cancer diagnosis or living with a debilitating chronic illness may experience 'some of the realities of hopelessness – feelings of sadness, loss, grief, or inability to escape or change a particular situation' (p.26). This intermediate level is distinguishable from the pathological level because, while

> persons whose hope is challenged may experience feelings of hopelessness, these feelings are more transitory in nature: With mobilization of resources they can be dealt with, and they often result in enhanced physical, mental, and spiritual functioning or quality of life. (Farran *et al.* 1995, p.26)

In contrast to both 'pathological hope' and 'challenged hope', Farran *et al.* discern hope structured as either 'unchallenged' by life experience, which they describe as having 'non-specific goals that have a good probability of happening' (p.17), or as 'ultimate hope', which they characterise as 'more closely tied to the experiential attribute of hope associated with "trial, captivity, and suffering"' (p.17). As they explain:

> Individuals often deal with hope in a more superficial or hypothetical manner until they experience stressful or difficult life experiences, such as a life-threatening illness or accident, that challenge the basic core of their existence and have an uncertain eventual outcome. (Farran *et al.* 1995, p.17)

For Farran *et al.*, 'ultimate hope' represents 'one's highest, deepest hope' (p.17).

'Ultimate hope' bears comparison with Gabriel Marcel's (2010) concept of 'absolute' hope, on which Garrard and Wrigley draw to argue that hope can and does change for people facing despair. Marcel's account of hope is informed by the parallels he identified between the captivity experiences of First World War prisoners and illness, the sense 'of being caught by the human condition' (Pruyser 1963, p.87). For Marcel, absolute hope becomes possible when, and only when, an individual is threatened with despair, which he characterises as having three central features. First, becoming 'so absorbed by the idea of one's own destruction that it is all that is anticipated' (Garrard and Wrigley 2009, p.40). Such a response leads to abandoning a 'sense of personal self' and an over-identification with 'the adverse outcome' (p.40). Second, experiencing time as 'closed' to any new possibility in which 'the passing of time becomes an impatient waiting for [the] end' (p.40). Third, the 'turning inwards of oneself to focus only on the inevitable' and 'abandoning involvement with other people' (p.41).

According to Pruyser (1963),[3] Marcel distinguishes hope phenomenologically from, for example, wishing and dreaming in that wishes and dreams have specific objects while hoping is more vague and diffuse 'in the sense that it has only a global object' (p.87). In which case, absolute hope has nothing to do with optimism or wishful thinking, it is

> not an elegant drifting in leisure and comfort, as a tourist may do in a Venetian gondola. It is much more like steering a ship in a gale. Hoping is a singularly unsentimental and unromantic affair. It permits no departure from reality, otherwise it becomes illusion and delusion. (Pruyser 1963, p.92)

As such, absolute hope has more affinity with willing than wishing (p.91). But most significantly, becoming hopeful effects change within a person and their relation to reality; change that is profoundly spiritual:

> He [sic] appears to himself as being implied in a wider reality which transcends him… at the moment hoping sets in, the hoper begins to perceive reality as of larger scope than the one he has hitherto dealt with… hoping implies an internal battle with one's self-love, in the direction of reduced narcissism. (Pruyser 1963, pp.89, 93, 94)

According to Garrard and Wrigley (2009), what Marcel describes as absolute hope is radically divergent from the standard belief–desire paring account of hope. In contrast, absolute hope is 'an overall stance towards life', which recognises the inevitable yet remains open to the possibility of experience and 'involves hope in others' (p.41).

---

3   I am grateful to John Ehman, Network Convener for the Research Network of the Association for Clinical Pastoral Education, for directing me to Pruyser's work.

[Absolute] hope rises above the inevitability of one's fate and maintains one's integrity in the face of it. This means that hope is not crushed by the recognition of one's inevitable fate, but also does not struggle against it. Although it recognizes the inevitability of destruction it refuses to anticipate it in a self-obsessed way. Second, hope incorporates a view of time as open and filled with the possibility of experience. Third, hope refuses to turn inwards into solitude: it has a communal aspect, which involves hope in others. (Garrard and Wrigley 2009, p.41)

As ethicists, Garrard and Wrigley are rightly concerned to answer the ethical challenge that the standard account of hope poses. For them, construing hope in terms of absolute hope offers a way to resolve the problem because, while respect for autonomy may leave a dying person at risk of falling into despair, absolute hope is 'entirely congruent with protecting the welfare of the patient, as absolute hope is just what prevents the descent into despair' (p.41).

The strength to live hopefully

Recourse to Marcel's conception of hope neatly resolves the ethical dilemma as Garrard and Wrigley (2009) identify it; however, the reality of clinical practice is unlikely to be as unproblematic as their resolution implies. This is because, while they highlight the 'communal aspect' of hope, they underplay its subjective and interpersonal aspects, creating a perhaps unintended impression that absolute hope, with its 'open-eyed grasp of the inevitability of the undesired, sometimes catastrophic, outcome' (p.40), is available to anyone by dint of their own inner resource and heroic self-effort.

For Nekolaichuk et al. (1999), the 'elusive, intangible qualities of hope … are grounded in the uniqueness of experience' (p.592). In contrast to the two-tier models of hope typified by Farran et al. (1995), Nekolaichuk et al. (1999) propose structuring the experience of hope 'as a location in three dimensional space' (p.602). Their somewhat complex methodology produces a model that 'emphasises the personal intangible experience of hope within a multidimensional framework' of three interrelated dimensions:

personal, situational and interpersonal (Nekolaichuk and Bruera 1998, p.40). The advantages of this three-dimensional model are that it adds a layer of complexity missing from the conventional two-tier models and that it illustrates both the multi-factorial influences that bear upon a person's hope and the significance of subjectivity at play in becoming hopeful.

Levine (2007), a psychoanalytic group psychotherapist, articulates the complex and subjective structuring of hope operating at the level of the unconscious with regard to an individual's internal object relations. Levine describes the individual who has good internal objects as one who is able to experience 'mature hope' and so 'able to perceive and respond to new possibilities' (p.299); and while this individual may have unfulfilled, disappointed or even painful expectations, these are 'not equated with self-worth' (p.299). Over against 'mature hope', he contrasts 'idealised hope' as that which is experienced by 'a person with unstable self/object development' (p.299):

> The person who relies upon idealized hope has inadequate self-soothing and self-affirming functions... [He or she has] not successfully achieved a healthy resolution of the developmental period of illusion, maintains an excessive sense of omnipotence and magical control over the environment, and has difficulty recovering from periods of disillusionment... A person in this state can often live in isolation, having the idealized hope as the only form of emotional connection. (Levine 2007, pp.299, 300, 302)

The parallel with the individual who has fallen into despair is obvious (Garrard and Wrigley 2009) and the prospect of such a person achieving the kind of absolute hope described by Marcel seems poor, unless, as Levine (2007) suggests, they are able to experience 'surviving empathic failures' (p.302).

Absolute hope is not achieved by mere act of will, as Pruyser seems to infer (1963, p.91); instead, the strength to live hopefully is founded on relationship, which according to Erikson, originates in infancy. Describing his psychosocial model of epigenetic development, Erikson (1995) locates the earliest emergence of hope at the point at which the child learns by experience that it can 'let the mother out of sight without undue anxiety or rage, because she has become an inner certainty as well as an outer predictability' (p.222). Erikson's account of the infant's relationship resonates well with the kind of attachment Bowlby (2005a, indebted to Ainsworth) terms a 'secure base', the kind of secure attachment that inspires the confidence that 'there are one or more trusted persons who will come to their aid should difficulties arise' (p.125). For Erikson (1997), such confidence, when established, is an ego-strength: hope as 'expectant desire' (p.59).

In the context of end of life care, the idea that the strength to live hopefully originates in infancy may appear bleakly pessimistic, suggesting that a dying person's capacity to live hopefully in the face of their impending death has been determined already by their experiences in the nursery. However, Erikson (1997) holds out reparative possibilities when he suggests that, 'when endangered by all-too-desperate discomfort', the confidence and expectant desire that has been compromised by an insecure base may be 'restored by competent consolation' (p.60). This chimes with Bowlby's (2005b) observation that the first task of the therapeutic relationship is 'to provide the patient with a secure base from which he can explore the various unhappy and painful aspects of his life' (p.156). It also locates the reparative possibilities of 'competent consolation' in the kind of holding relationship described by Winnicott, a holding that contains the other and survives their negative transferences. (See Chapter 3, in connection with the chaplain as an accompanying presence.)

Building on the foundations of Bowlby's Attachment Theory, Stern's (1985) work on affective attunement and Heard and Lake's (1997) theory of the dynamics of attachment, McCluskey's (2005) research into the interactions between careseekers and caregivers underlines the reparative possibilities of caring relationships. According to McCluskey, 'The function of attachment behaviour is to ensure survival' (p.74): based on their most primitive experience, the infant builds an 'internal working model' (Bowlby 1998) of their self in relation to attachment figures, which are stored as models for predicting how such relationships might work in the future. McCluskey's research offers a framework for understanding how careseekers and caregivers interact when anxious, under stress or frightened. She argues that, in these conditions:

> what we need is a response that puts us in touch with our competence to act; with our emotional, physical and intellectual capacity. A response which enables us to identify people we can rely on, as well as our spiritual, financial and aesthetic resources. And if we are severely incapacitated this response must also feel related to us, be sensitive, alert and responsible and above all focused on our well-being. (McCluskey 2005, p.3)

In other words, people dealing with situations of existential threat need help to mobilise their own inner resources and, according to McCluskey, the keys to this are the ongoing support of a secure or 'safe base', but more importantly, an other who is capable of demonstrating empathic attunement (p.76).

Because she is working from within Attachment Theory, McCluskey is oriented to the idea that adults who are frightened or otherwise existentially threatened will seek and respond to care in ways that accord to their internal working models of attachment. This means that a dying person will seek to attach to a caregiver in ways that *are* determined by their nursery experiences; in other words, as a careseeker, they will form attachments to caregivers in one of the ways identified by Ainsworth (1991): secure attachments; insecure ambivalent attachments; insecure avoidant attachments; or disorganised attachments (McCluskey 2005, p.3). However, it does not mean that those whose styles of attachment are anything other than secure will not benefit from the attachment relationship. According to McCluskey two factors make the difference: (1) whether the person offering care can do so *empathically*; and (2) whether they can maintain their empathic stance 'over time and *for as long as is necessary*' (p.77, emphasis added). Intuitively, this is the kind of relationship chaplains offer.

Presence and the reconfiguring of hope

It is no surprise, therefore, that hope researchers consistently stress the importance of human relationship for people who are dying.

Chi's (2007) analysis of the literature finds that the importance of 'affirming relationships', 'positive relationships with professional caregivers' and 'supportive family or friends' rated highly in five out of seven of the research projects she identifies as addressing 'the strategies patients used to maintain hope' (p.421). Rumbold (1986) identifies strong supportive relationships with other persons as 'common to all cases where there is a hopeful acceptance of death' (p.70), and 'interpersonal connectedness' topped Herth's (1990) seven categories of hope-fostering strategies (p.1254), which her participants described as '"the feeling that the person is truly present with me", "the touch or hug that communicates 'I'm with you'"' (p.1254). Herth's findings have been replicated by Buckley and Herth (2004), who relate a poignant interview with a man who had previously 'claimed to have no spiritual beliefs and felt that death was "the end"'.

> The researcher visited him a second time when he was in the hospice days before his death. He was restless and appeared frightened. His family did not visit him and he turned his friends away. He said hope was still important to him, but it was becoming 'less and less accessible'.
> (Buckley and Herth 2004, p.37)

Although Buckley and Herth include this incident under their hope fostering category of 'spirituality/having faith', it could perhaps more appropriately feature in their hope hindering category of 'abandonment and isolation'.

The chaplains I interviewed seem intuitively to understand the importance of presence in fostering hopefulness. Several chaplains expressed the idea that being-*with* a dying person who is without hope effectively says to them, 'You're not alone; there is someone with you'. One spoke of 'the kind of black despair in which the only way to help someone is to enter it with them and to stay with it'; she described herself as being 'used to sitting in the pits with people and not trying to change it for them' (CHP005.01). Speaking about her work with a woman she met in day hospice, she went on to say:

> I think I was able to be present because I wasn't trying to change anything for her, and that we connected as

human beings, one who was deeply suffering and very angry, met by a human being who accepted all that and didn't try to change any of it because I can't. And to try to make it better would only have made it worse. (CHP005.07)

For her, being with people in the hard and difficult place is far from hope-less:

I don't see it as hopeless work at all. I suppose, starting from the baseline that I cannot give people hope, but I can be with people without any kind of hope in a way that is helpful and comforting and, perhaps, strengthening for them… So, staying with people in the darkness is not a hope-less situation, because I think, in the process of grief, working with people in that pre-death, pre-bereavement work, I see it as (more for the person who's dying), a support and a love, and to be loved when you are without hope is something that is actually beautiful. (CHP005.08)

That a chaplain might admit that she 'wasn't trying to change anything' for a person suffering spiritual pain, or even that she might find something of beauty in the situation, may seem incongruous if not actually perverse to healthcarers whose professional *raison d'être* is concerned with trying to relieve the painful experience of a suffering other. However, of all healthcare professionals, palliative care chaplains are the least best placed to effect material change, and perhaps because they understand there is *nothing* they can *do* to change a dying person's situation, they understand that it is their being-*with* that matters. One chaplain expressed it graphically:

All chaplains have to offer is themselves, if you like. There's a cartoon … where the doctor goes in with the stethoscope, and the nurse goes in with her drugs and the chaplain goes in stark naked because that's all they have to offer. (CHP003.18)

The point is not that being-*with* is the sole prerogative of chaplains; but that being-*with* is *all* that a chaplain has to offer: the *only* tool a chaplain has in the bag, so to speak, is their own self – the quality of their ability to be a being-*with*. This is both the challenge chaplains face as spiritual carers – 'what makes it a hard and painful and difficult job to do' (CHP003.18) – and the privileged opportunity they have that is very often denied to their colleagues due to the practical demands of modern healthcare. As one chaplain put it:

> I think all the other disciplines can do it, but find it more difficult because, on the whole, they have things to do to make things a little bit better: a syringe driver, a different prescription, some care of a stoma bag or whatever it might be; some help with mobility aids or some oils for a massage. We have none of that to rely on, so we only have ourselves to rely on. (CHP005.07)

Observing that 'a very important aspect for the chaplain [is] to be present in whatever way is appropriate in that moment for that person' (CHP005.07), this chaplain articulated what many of the interviewees also expressed: the idea that spiritual care is being-*with* another person in the way that allows that person to be the person that they need to be.

> I was asked to see a patient in the community who was close to the end of his life. I don't know why I was asked to go as opposed to a counsellor, because what I was asked to do was to go and try and facilitate a conversation between him and his wife, because his wife just wanted to talk over the top of him all the time to stop him saying what he felt he needed to say. And when I got there he was watching football – and that was fine ('cos I've got teenaged sons, so I know about football). And then we talked about the fact that he was having to sleep downstairs, 'cos he couldn't get up stairs; and then it was that actually he wasn't sleeping, 'cos he was laying in bed thinking about things. And when I said, 'And how do you feel about the things that you're thinking about?' And there was a huge pause – I was praying his wife wasn't going to interrupt – and suddenly it just all came out, all of the fears, all the anxieties. He began with, 'Well, I'm here, and I'm gonna be here; and being here is okay, but it's getting from here to here that's the frightening thing.' And he poured all of his fears out.

And at the end of it, without even stopping, he looked at me and he said, 'You're the first person who's let me do that. They come in and they ask about my bowels and my back and my pain, and nobody says, "And how is it for you?"' So that, I think, is what we're about. And some other staff can also do that, and do it, but they are seen with their professional badge on and we're seen as ... we haven't got an axe to grind on symptoms or whatever, and we're not gonna be suggesting that we change the medication or ... we're just there to, to listen. (CHP003.18)

From my conversations with interviewees, a chaplain's presence is not perceived quite as neutrally as this chaplain appears to imply. As her colleague makes clear:

Being present – it sounds quite an inactive thing to be, but it's actually a very proactive thing 'to be present', it's very active, it's, it's a very dynamic thing to be. (CHP005.03)

Something of that dynamism is evident in the extended extract that follows. Asked to give examples of his work in practice, this chaplain related stories about people with whom he had worked: a religious woman, who was 'shit-scared of dying', and two men with no particular beliefs. What is striking was the way in which, intuitively, he evidenced what for McCluskey are the two factors that make the difference: empathic attunement and the ability to stay with them 'for as long as is necessary'.

I can remember a lady who asked to see me, who was actually quite a senior official in her church. And I went to see her and I said, 'What can I do for you?' And she said, 'I'm shit-scared of dying'. I said, 'Why? You've been a church member all your life, and doesn't your faith support you? Doesn't your belief support you?' She said, 'That's the problem!' She said, 'Only now, now I've got this terminal diagnosis, have I really thought about it; and only now do I really realise that all my life I've been doing church and religion and I don't actually know, or have a relationship with God.' So we had about two weeks to try and re-look at her journey in another way that would make sense to her – not me telling her what my experience was, but for her to really explore what her faith was about, or her lack of faith.

... she had a good knowledge of Scripture and I think I was able to take her back through Scripture in a way that would, kind of make it accessible and more real and more understandable. And then to link that with helping her find a new way of praying that maybe wasn't a list of requirements or words even, to take her into silence and to experiencing God in a new way for her. And to be touched at that level is to be touched, not cerebrally, but spiritually – God speaks from spirit to spirit, to our spirit and we still try and do a lot of that in our head, and you can't do it that way. I think that was where she was: she was a very bright lady, she was very cerebral and she hadn't realised that, actually, we commune at a different level, in a different way, and that way is the way that will sustain you when your, when your brain is saying, 'I'm shit-scared,' which is where she started from.

... I like to try and meet people where they are, at their point of need. For that lady, 'I'm shit-scared' was her initial point of need and so, from that, I would say, 'Well, I don't want you to be afraid; I want you to know some of the peace that maybe I have.'

Another gentleman, who was clerked in as agnostic, I went to see him and, he was a young man, I said he might think it funny to get a visit from the chaplain, "Cos I know you're clerked in as agnostic.' And he said, 'Yeah, I s'pose so!' I said, 'Well, in the hospice there's an awful lot of women in here and you may just want a bit of bloke chat, you may just want a friend for the time you're in here.' And I think he was grateful that I wasn't giving him anything 'religious' or spiritual. And he – you know when people look at you in the eyes and they grab your attention – and he said, 'Yeah, I'd really like that.' For him, all he wanted was a friend, somebody who was going to be there for him, not take him anywhere he didn't want to be.

And I remember another guy who came in eventually as an in-patient ... and he was not so well. And he again, didn't have any particular beliefs and he didn't particularly want to go anywhere with it. He was into sailing, he was into fast cars and he liked a pint, and that's what we did: we went out in our fast cars (laughs), we'd go down to the pub and have a pint, and we'd talk. And sometimes the conversation would come round to, you know, his TVR and how many miles per gallon it didn't do (laughs). There would be practical bits about how he was trying to set his wife, his family and the financial bits up. Then we'd just have a laugh. But when he was dying, and he died at home, I was one of the last people he called; and I went to see him and we'd talk, and we didn't talk anything about God, we didn't do a prayer, I didn't give him a blessing, he just wanted something of my presence, and for me that was enough as well, and it was clearly enough for him.

... Maybe I represented something that – maybe he wanted to be with the person who was going to do his funeral service for him, 'cos I said I would do that for him and we'd discussed the style and what he would like. I think some people do find us a comfort and maybe they don't understand exactly what that is. And I think that's something to do with the fact that we are all spiritual people; that within us is, what I would describe as a very deep well and right at the bottom of the well is, if you like, the water of life, and we, kind of, know that but we've never really looked deep enough into that to draw from it; and maybe they see something of that water in us; maybe it's a little bit higher, further up the walls of the well and more easily reached ... I think there is something of that. In the same way as when I was a novice ... if you were a restless young novice, in chapel they would kneel you next to an old peaceful monk and the peace, or the aura, or whatever you'd like to call it that radiated from him you would sit in – a bit like the ripples of a pool – and something of that person settled you. And I think there's something of that about what we have that we can offer, without words but with presence. I'm sure that's very different for other people, but for me that makes sense. (CHP101.08–.11)

Summary
Unlike other healthcare professionals, chaplains do not identify hope-fostering as an explicit aspect of their care for people who are dying. However, they do regard hope-fostering as a valuable outcome of their work, one that is engendered by their presence rather than anything they may actually say or do. As such, hope-fostering is an unsought-for, but nonetheless not entirely unexpected outcome of a chaplain's being-*with*.

Working with the transferential projections – positive or negative – to the point of being accepted as an accompanier; demonstrating their preparedness to stay-*with* those for whom they care, *no-matter-what*. Attending to the soul of the dying other by sharing something of their experience, containing and surviving it: in these ways chaplains comfort (*confortare*) those for whom they care and consequently support them to be hopeful, not now concerned with the future of desire unfulfilled, but as a being-*towards*-life, open to connectedness and possibility – their hope reconfigured to 'hope in the present'.

Rumbold (1986) hypothesised 'that without such a relationship hope ... is extremely unlikely to emerge' (p.70). It may not be too incautious to speak of the power of presence to reconfigure hope, and to suggest that the chaplain's presence can help effect such reconfiguration.

Chapter 6

Rethinking Spiritual Care as *Presence*

What stands out clearly from the previous chapters is that *presence* is of fundamental importance to the practice of spiritual care. And the implication of this is that, when it comes to working with people who are dying, a chaplain's most significant 'tool' is not their religious knowledge or their liturgical skill, but *who they are in themselves* and their ability to offer their *presence* – their being-*with* – which may in itself help a dying person be hopeful.

This invites an obvious question: if presence is of such fundamental importance to spiritual care, then what does it actually mean to be present to a person who knows they are dying? To put it more specifically: what does it mean to be present to a person who is navigating between hope (*sperare*) and despair (*desperare*)? This is the question Daniel posed me when I met him (see Chapter 1) at the point where he, as a young man, was facing prematurely the imminent certainty of his own death, and with it the existential reality of his own non-existence. The silent tears he shed as we sat together in the dim quiet of his hospice side-room were tears of loss: for those he would be leaving and for the many ambitions he would never achieve. They were also tears of fear; the visceral expression of Daniel's awakening to his own death anxiety.

Managing the anxiety of death

Writing in 1926, Heidegger understood death anxiety to be *the* issue that defines our being as humans. According to Heidegger (1962), most of us live, most of the time, with the idea that death is an unpleasant fact of life; but equally, we live with it as a fact that has little bearing on *my life at the moment*. As such, death is but a 'well-known event occurring within-the-world' (p.297) about which we talk

> in a 'fugitive' manner, either expressly or else in a way which is mostly inhibited, as if to say, 'One of these days one will die too, in the end; but right now it has nothing to do with us.' (Heidegger 1962, p.297)

In other words, although we may talk freely, in an everyday way, about death and dying, in most cases we are speaking about death as the death of others, and in that way we insulate ourselves against the terrifying idea that *we ourselves will die and (at least physically) will cease to be.*

The existential certainty of our own non-existence is simply too much to bear and Heidegger details some of the strategies we deploy with the intent of defending ourselves against the anxiety that our non-existence provokes. For example, Heidegger identifies 'evasive concealment' as a strategy in which 'the "neighbours" often still keep talking the "dying person" into the belief that he will escape death and soon return to the tranquillised everydayness of the world of his concern' (p.297). Although they intend these words to console the person who is dying, the effect is to insulate them against fear of their death. Or again, Heidegger speaks of 'tranquillisation' as a strategy akin to a form of non-medical terminal sedation, the subtle application of 'evasive concealment', intended now 'not only for him who is "dying" but just as much for those who "console" him' (p.298).

Perhaps the most pernicious of the defensive, insulating strategies Heidegger observes is 'alienation', which cuts a dying person off from their own experience. The strategy of 'alienation' projects the view that thinking about death is in some way an unhealthy preoccupation: 'a cowardly fear, a sign of insecurity ... a sombre way of fleeing from the world' (p.298). In any case, thinking about death is to be discouraged and well-intentioned friends, family and healthcarers reinterpret such thoughts about death as 'fear in the face of an oncoming event' (p.298) – a thing more manageable than facing death anxiety. According to Heidegger, all that is acceptable to those caring for a dying person is an 'indifferent tranquillity as to the "fact" that one dies'. However, the result of such stoic indifference is that the dying person becomes alienated from their own experience of their own dying, distanced from their 'ownmost non-relational potentiality-for-Being' (p.298). As Heidegger concludes, we concede 'the "certainty" of death ... just in order to weaken that certainty by covering up dying' (p.300).

Those who work daily with dying people observe such insulating strategies; they are a part of what Heidegger regards as inauthentic everydayness; but, however inauthentic these protective strategies may be, healthcarers need to treat them with respect. Penny's strategy for managing her death anxiety was typical of a sophisticated strategy observed in some people; a strategy that can be particularly frustrating for healthcarers who feel it is important to speak openly and 'get the patient on board'.

Penny: 'If I could get control of my emotions ... everything would be fine'

'I'm spiritual not religious.'

Penny explained that she had been brought up to believe, but that she had experienced 'traumas' in her life that had made her 'see things differently'. She said she had had a difficult mother, who had told her that she had only come into the world, 'Because her father was a dirty old man.' She spoke about the abuse she received from her mother – although not what had become of her father – and how she herself had married a man who had treated her in a similar way. And she described her childhood strategy for dealing with traumatic situations.

'As a child, I had a place in my mind where I would go until things became safe again.'

'Sounds like that was a safe place to go.'

'Mmm ... I need it now, but I've lost it ... I can't find it.'

Penny spoke of being a rational, practical person, who didn't allow her emotions to get involved. She apologised for being emotional now. Then she spoke about a little dog she had as a child, a Jack Russell, of whom she was particularly fond.

'I used to train it every day. One day I came home from school and found my mother was giving him away. She said it was because I loved him.' She paused. 'I'd give anything to have that dog with me now.'

Again she apologised for being 'teary'.

After this, Penny went on to speak about being in control, about her practical nature, and about making preparations for the future. She wanted no funeral and intended for her body to be donated to 'medical science'. She had made a will, and was happy for her children to make the arrangements for her to go into a nursing home.

'If I could only get control of my emotions then everything would be fine.'

She remained in control of the rest of our conversation, which she took away from the emotive and focused more on practical things.

Over the days, I discovered that Penny had spoken to other members of the multidisciplinary team. Doctors, nurses and social work colleagues were all hearing Penny's story – or parts of it – and picking up on her distress. As such, she was generating a degree of concern among the rest of the team, to the extent that her consultant was beginning to suggest it might be possible to extend her stay beyond the period her specialist palliative needs strictly required, just in order to try to help her find some psychospiritual peace.

I continued to visit Penny as often as possible, at times daily.

Sometimes she spoke about her children and their partners. Sometimes she spoke about her creativity – which she (and I) regarded as spiritual and which she channelled into her hobbies; she spoke particularly about her pleasure in woodworking and her fondness of old carpenters' tools. On these occasions, I just listened.

Sometimes she spoke about her life. She never really said much more about herself than she told me at our first meeting, and as she approached the threshold of her tears, she would catch herself, apologise and recover her composure, before moving on to less emotive, more secure ground. On these occasions, I would gently, tentatively suggest that she might find it helpful to talk more about her feelings; but Penny always declined any engagement in any type of counselling or psychospiritual work.

'If I could only get control of my emotions then everything would be fine.'

As I spoke with Penny and with colleagues about her, it seemed to me, that she *was* in control – that she was managing the telling of her story in a piecemeal way that ensured, as far as she possibly could, that everything remained fine. Whether this was conscious or otherwise, Penny was chopping her story into orderly episodes and giving certain episodes to certain people, in a way that confounded her professional healthcarers.

It is interesting to reflect that, as a child, Penny had created a place in her mind where she would go 'until things became safe again'. In other words, she had learned to compartmentalise. And although she claimed she had since lost that place, as she approached her death, Penny was again compartmentalising in order to manage and retain control over the emotions that threatened to overwhelm her. Perhaps in this way she was able to bear what otherwise might have been an unbearable despair and at the same time find a way to let go of at least some of the baggage she needed to free herself from.

It is important to be clear that insulating strategies are a form of psychological defence that, as Winnicott (1954a) points out, can be regarded as 'normal phenomenon that can properly be studied in the healthy person' (p.281). It is, therefore, an incautious healthcarer who attempts to 'steal' the defence mechanisms of a suffering other; a 'theft' that Levine (1986) calls 'an act of righteousness and separatism' (p.163) and which we might consider a form of psychospiritual abuse.

Owning the anxiety of our own death

In trying to answer the question, What does it mean to be present to a person who is navigating between hope (*sperare*) and despair (*desperare*)? I am suggesting that what matters is the healthcarer's, and particularly the chaplain's, ability to be emotionally available – to be a being-*with* – a person who is more or less consciously living in the anxieties of their own death.

However, this kind of being-*with* is not as straightforward as we might wish it to be. The complexity of the caring relationship is such that the death anxiety of the person who is *being cared for* is likely to provoke the latent death anxieties of the person *doing the caring*. The equation is very simple: caring for people who are dying confronts healthcarers with the reality of our own death. This is all but unavoidable and it presents healthcarers with a profound psychospiritual challenge. Out of our desire to care we have chosen to work with the very people whose present and lived experience exposes us daily to the darkest of all our terrors: the certainty that we, along with every other living person, have instinctively defended ourselves against *all our lives*.

Being present, being *fully* present, being a being-*with*, involves something of a paradox: as healthcarers, we have a strong urge to care that compels us to give ourselves to others; however, at the same time, the dying others for whom we care provoke in us an anxiety that compels us to withhold ourselves. Internally conflicted in the existential 'tug-of-love' between these competing compulsions, it is understandable that we would seek some form of psychospiritual protection, for example, adopting the form of insulating strategy that Heidegger (1962) describes as 'alienation'. In this case, trying to protect our[real]self by hiding it away behind the mask of our[professional]self, we effectively split ourselves in two and risk performing our healthcarer role in much the same way as an actor performs a theatrical role. However, while the idea that we can leave our[real]selves at home and send our[professional]selves off to work each day may provide an insulating defence against the threat of our death anxiety, as Heidegger points out, it only results in alienating us from our own lived experience.

In terms of being fully present, the point here is that, when as healthcarers we hide our[real]selves behind the role of our[professional]selves, we effectively hold back our[real]selves from being-*with* the person who is dying. In which case, we abandon them to die in isolation. Harvard psychologist turned-spiritual teacher, Ram Dass expresses well the problem this poses for spiritual care:

> I started to hang out with more and more people who were dying and just learning to listen and be with them, and listen not only to how I could be there for them, realising that all I could bring to them, finally, was my truth. I couldn't bring rule books about how to be with dying people. When I walked into a room with a person who was dying, there was just the person and me, and here we are. And if I'm full of hiding in roles and identities I cut myself off from them and they're left

alone, *which is the hardest way to die.* (Dass 1992, emphasis added)

The challenge of being fully present to, of being a being-*with*, a dying person is, first and foremost, the challenge of being a being-*with* to ourselves. As Ram Dass memorably phrased it in his 1970s counter-culture book, the challenge is to *Be Here Now* (1971). This is the challenge of being congruent to our own lived experience in the present moment. In terms of caring for a dying person, being present to ourselves *here now* means recognising and *owning* our own anxiety about death and allowing that death anxiety to inform, but not intrude upon, our being-*with* a dying other.

Insisting that recognising and *owning* our death anxiety is of vital importance in caring spiritually for a dying person poses a serious ethical challenge to those like McSherry (2001) who want to reclaim what he sees as the traditional role of nurses as spiritual carers. For McSherry, 'nurses are the rightful custodians of all matters spiritual' (p.107), a claim that he bases on the fact that nursing developed historically from within the religious institutions of the medieval Christian period. It is a matter of interpretation as to whether such an exalted claim remains warranted. If it is, modern nurses are being expected to offer care in an area for which they (unlike their medieval monastic forebears) are not equipped, either by training or (in many cases) by disposition. In contrast, the medieval forebears of modern nurses would have spent a great deal of time and spiritual energy facing death and contemplating their own death as an integral part of their spiritual practice and formation. So the ethical question this poses is: To what extent is it right to expect modern nurses (who are largely non-religious or secular) to confront directly their own personal death anxiety in order that they can care for physically ill and dying people?

In fact, McSherry (2006) pushes the ethical envelope much further. Defining spirituality in terms of 'a search for meaning and purpose' (p.53), he declares that it is 'the health care professionals' role to assist individuals to make sense and find meaning in such times of crisis such as the acceptance of a terminal diagnosis' (p.54). Leaving aside the appropriateness of defining spirituality as a search for meaning and purpose (Nolan 2011), McSherry's assertion needs to question how ethical is it to demand that nurses fulfil a role that is more suited to that of a suitably qualified spiritual advisor or guide, or an accredited counsellor or psychotherapist?

There is no question that McSherry is right when he points to the fact that nurses 'hold a unique position in the delivery of patient care' (2001, p.109), and his recent research indicates that the majority of nurses 'believe providing spiritual care enhances the overall quality of nursing care' (McSherry and Jamieson 2011, p.1765). However, his recent work also points out the extent to which 'many nurses … feel that they lack sufficient educational preparedness in meeting their patients' spiritual needs' (p.1763).

In the nursing literature, attempts to address this need for guidance appear to concern questions of definition and assessment: what *is* spiritual need and how is it to be recognised? McSherry (2001) has himself noted that spiritual assessment tools come charged with an inherent irony, in so far as they have the potential to dehumanise spiritual care by reducing 'the assessment of spirituality to a mechanistic or "tick box" exercise' (p.111). It is possible that this preoccupation with measuring and recording is just one more development in the process of what Paley (2008a) terms 'nursification', a process that facilitates the nursing 'profession' to accrue professional power and jurisdiction over 'a particular occupational territory' (p.181). It is also possible that preoccupation with assessment is one more strategy intended to insulate nurses from their sense of empty helplessness in the face of death. In this case, 'distraction activity' is an understandable, but ultimately ineffective attempt at filling this sense of personal helplessness with a sense of professional purpose.

Sue: I'd love to have my nails done!

For the previous eight weeks, Sue had been battered by both her illness and the health services that had been caring for her. She looked world-weary and drained, and I knew I wouldn't be staying long.

I introduced myself and we exchanged a few politenesses before Sue gently let me know that she 'wasn't really religious'. As per normal when I hear those words, I explained that my role was to be supportive and that if there was anything I could do, I'd be happy to help. I prepared to leave.

'There is something.' I paused, eager to be of use. 'I was going to have my nails done when I was in the hospital, but the person who was going to do it didn't show up, and then I found out I was coming in here. If there's any chance of getting my nails done, I'd be really grateful!'

I was on the job! I went straight to the Ward Clerk – 'There's a volunteer who comes on Fridays ... put Sue's name in the book.'

That was it, job done! Easy, and easily rewarding. Except that the volunteer – being a volunteer – just *might* not be in this Friday. I went back to Sue to report on our success ... and possible failure!

'Thanks. That's great.'

But not quite great enough for me. So when I stumbled on a different volunteer doing the nails of another person, I pounced and tried to book her for Sue.

'Yes', she was able to see Sue; and 'Yes', she could see her today.

Excellent! Except, when this different volunteer arrived at Sue's door, it was firmly closed behind a nurse attending to Sue's care. Nothing left, but to wait and see if Plan A would work.

℘

Friday, 9.30 am. I pass my original nail volunteer on the stairs.

'Jane, Hi! I don't know if you've got time today, but if you have, there's a lady in Room 17 who would love to have her nails done.'

'Yes I know! I saw her name in the book!'

'You're a star! She'll really appreciate that. Thanks.'

Later in the day, I looked in on Sue.

'Did you get your nails done?'

'Yes, she came earlier. Thanks for arranging that.'

I walked out pleased that I had effected some small difference and organised some small comfort for this worn and wearied woman.

℘

And then I began to wonder: Why it had mattered so much? Why had I taken on this small task as such a personal project? Why had it mattered so to me that *I* follow it up? Why wasn't it enough for me that I'd put her name on the list? If the volunteer could help, she would and, as it turned out, she did; she would have helped whether or not I had made it my personal crusade. Why was I so concerned?

Not for Sue. Not really.

I could see that she was in need of a little healing balm; after her tough experiences over the last two months, she needed a little TLC. But no more than did so many other people. Why was I so concerned to do this simple thing for her?

If not for Sue, then who?

Probably for me.

Definitely for me.

Perhaps, in Sue's need for a manicure, I saw an opportunity to feel that I was *doing something* for once, albeit something quite meagre. Perhaps in taking ownership of her small problem I was in some way trying to take control of that vague sense I often feel that, in the face of so much suffering, I'm just not doing very much; that vague but persistent feeling of anxious *uselessness*.

... In being there for others – who so often don't understand what it is that I'm supposed to be there *for* (even after I've been there for them!) – I sometimes find myself wondering what it is that I *am* there for.

... In offering myself to another to be there for what they need, I am actually putting the meaning of what I do into their hands – the hands of people who are just too weak to play at being nice, too weary to be politely grateful. I am putting the meaning of what I do into the hands of people who are unselfconsciously direct – and in that way putting something of the meaning of who I am into the hands of another of those who are too fragile to notice my need. I'm waiting for them to give value to my being-*there* for them, waiting for them to validate my presence, and sometimes they're just too weak to do it. And to be honest, sometimes they just don't value it at all.

So, sometimes it's just easier – sometimes it's a lot easier – to *do-something-for* someone than to keep on trying to *be-someone-with* someone.

Saunders (1996) warns that this 'feeling of helplessness may urge us to withdraw or to escape into a zealous hyperactivity which can well exacerbate the patient's suffering' (p.11).

Withdrawal and escape are understandable responses when we are confronted by a dying other who threatens to trigger our own death anxiety. It seems important, then, that anyone involved in helping people prepare spiritually to die should devote some time to working on their own death anxiety.

Yalom (2008) has written about facing our death anxiety from the perspective of Existential psychotherapy and he borrows a maxim from the 17th-century French aristocrat, François de la Rochefoucauld (2007), that likens thinking about death to staring at the sun: 'You cannot stare straight into the face of the sun, or death' (Yalom 2008, title page). Although he does not encourage anyone to stare at the sun, Yalom is an advocate for the idea that, *'though the physicality of death destroys us, the idea of death saves us'* (p.7). By this, he means that 'the tranquillised everydayness' yields, as Heidegger (1962) identifies, to the anticipation that death is one's *'ownmost possibility'* (pp.297, 303). Yalom's (1980) important point is that the shift needs to be made from everyday *'forgetfulness of being'* to the 'state of *mindfulness of being'* (pp.30–1). In many cases, this shift is effected by what he terms 'awakening experiences' (2008, p.36), the kind of 'jolting, irreversible experience which shifts the individual from the everyday mode to a more authentic mode', of which 'death is by far the most potent' (Yalom 2000, p.11). However, he also offers advice, intended for psychotherapists but equally appropriate for healthcarers, aimed at enabling those willing to stare at the sun to do so safely. (For other writers who offer their own perspective on developing a 'state of *mindfulness of being'* see, for example, Hanh (1993; 2002) and Levine (1986).)

The point is that recognising and owning our own death anxiety is a necessary and important preparation for anyone who is serious about spiritual care; and it is particularly important for those who are caring spiritually for a person who is dying. However, as de la Rochefoucauld (2007) says: 'You cannot stare straight into the face of the sun, or death' – it is too painful, and we are quick to look away from either.

Returning to Daniel

Walking into Daniel's room (see Chapter 1), it was deceptively easy for me to 'forget' the enormity of his impending reality, to 'forget' the fact that this young man's life was coming to its certain end. I could easily 'excuse' my 'forgetting': I was, after all, preoccupied with the weight of my own agitation about what and how I should be with Daniel – Would I be what he needed? If not, would he send me away? Would I be embarrassed in front of my professional colleagues because I had failed him? Would I fail myself, and be embarrassed in front of him?

At the time, these seemed like pressing questions, but with the unhurried objectivity of hindsight, they were a complete irrelevance. Certainly, they were an irrelevance for Daniel. On reflection, they were the displacement of my anxieties about my own death, which he was provoking in me. In that moment, it was easier for me to own my anxiety about how Daniel would react to me than it was to own my anxiety about how I was reacting to death, whose approach was beginning to permeate Daniel's room. In that moment, it was easier for me to worry about my potential failure as a professional than it was to 'stare straight into the face of the sun'.

Daniel's invitation to join him was more than I had anticipated. It was a most intimate invitation: to be with him right there among his unspoken anxieties; to be in a place with him that he had not unlocked even to his close family.

Daniel used words to speak about his concern that his treatment was not being effective; but as he struggled to say what he was unable to say, he used undiluted emotion to express himself directly into my soul. In those moments with Daniel, I had no place to indulge the narcissistic vanities that had earlier distracted me. Daniel's emotional communication compelled me into being-*with* him, present there in his soul-space. Without words, Daniel spoke to me about his growing realisation that he was dying; and my experience, in that moment, was *something* of how that felt. That experience has stayed with me, and I try now to let it inform my being-*with* those others I meet who lie in Daniel's place. I said almost nothing and, as we sat *with* each other, my sense was that we both understood clearly what it was that Daniel had not said.

Being with Daniel in the intensity of the few moments we spent together opened me to begin learning more about what it means to offer spiritual care to a dying person. Talking with palliative care chaplains has expanded this learning, which I would summarise in four points, which are my attempt to answer the question that began this chapter. Offering a dying person spiritual care, means:

recognising and owning one's personal anxiety about death and, crucially, being able to hold that anxiety in such a way that it can inform, but not intrude upon, one's being-*with* a person who is dying – this is a form of what some call '*mindfulness of being*'

attending to the other, which starts with listening actively to what they have to say – with and without words – but is really more about giving oneself to the other *for the time you are together* – in other words, giving the other as much of yourself as you can bear, fully being-*with* the other

staying-with the other, being able and willing to go all the way together along that part of their journey the other will invite you to share

being open to change within oneself at a personal, spiritual level – spiritual care is not an intervention one can *do* to an other in a way that is unconnected from them; spiritual care is all about connection, it is person-to-person communication, it can and will profoundly affect the carer as much as the one who is cared for.

Chapter 7

Towards a Theory of 'Chaplain as Hopeful Presence'

Summary

In preceding chapters, I described a series of 'moments' in the relationship between a chaplain and a person who is dying; these are discernable, organic moments rather than definite stages through which the relationship passes. Here, I want to summarise these moments as a theory of *chaplain as hopeful presence*, a presence that moves from transference loaded first contact to a hope enhancing relationship (Figure 7.1 see p.130).

Evocative presence

To begin with, a chaplain's presence is an *evocative presence*. Transference is an everyday part of life and, consequently, all human contact evokes some kind of transferential response, which may be either positive or negative. In psychotherapeutic terms, 'transference' describes how one person unconsciously projects onto another a set of thoughts, feelings, and expectations that belong to someone else in a different place and time.

The point is that chaplains are intuitively aware that their presence evokes both positive and negative transferential projections in those for whom they care and in each case the *outcome* will be positive or negative.

For example, when a person requests a chaplain, the chaplain can expect to be the object of positive transferential phantasies. The person requesting the visit is likely to be 'delighted' (CHP001.02) to see the chaplain: they may gain a sense of security from being with someone they think shares their beliefs and so understands their needs; or they may associate the chaplain with positive memories linked to their 'residual faith' or their childhood. These are *positive outcomes* from positive transferential projections. However, some religiously minded people may so idealise the chaplain that they feel they have to be on their best behaviour. As a consequence, they may feel unable to disclose 'their real feelings and their real thoughts about God' (CHP103.04), and the result will be a *negative outcome*.

When chaplains routinely visit, or when they are referred to a person by another healthcarer, they can be less certain that they will be the object of a positive transference. They are just as likely to be the object of that person's negative transferential projection and encounter apathy, antipathy or (rarely) undisguised hostility. *Strong negative transferences* seem always to have *negative outcomes*; however, with a little gentle persistence, even the response, 'Bugger off, I don't want to talk to you!' (CHP004.07) can result in an outcome in which the dying person feels valued and accepted. Key to achieving a *positive outcome* is the chaplain's ability to deconstruct the logic of the judgemental religious phantasy:

> the chaplain represents God,
> God is judgemental,
>> therefore the chaplain will be judgemental.

Deconstructing this logic is possible if and where chaplains stay-*with* the negative transference, when they 'accept' or 'receive' the negative projection, yet at the same time resist it by contradicting the person's expectation of how the chaplain will be:

> the chaplain represents God,
> the chaplain accepts me as I am,
>> therefore God might (after all) accept me as I am.

In this way, chaplains demonstrate that they are willing and able to be in human contact with the suffering person *no-matter-what*, and at this point their relationship has the potential to become creatively therapeutic.

Accompanying presence

Once the chaplain has accepted and worked with the dying person's transferential projection, the chaplain may become an *accompanying presence*, someone who can and does stay-*with* the dying person. As such, chaplains have no therapeutic aim or professional agenda; they do not accompany in order to do something *to* or *for* those for whom they care, so much as simply to be someone *with* them.

In this way, chaplains intuitively understand the importance of 'dwelling' or being-*with* an other, without any well meaning agenda or intention to manipulate. Dwelling means accompanying the other, being-*with* them in a way that allows the other to be the being they are and need to be rather than the being anyone else, including the chaplain, may wish or need them to be. As such, accompanying extends to accepting the other person's right to die in his or her own way, rather than according to any prescribed model of what a 'good death' should be.

As an accompanier, the chaplain attends to the dying soul (*psyché*) who is at risk of losing hope, as Levinas puts it, 'facing the face in its mortality' with its 'summons', 'demands' and 'claims' (1989, p.125), in a way that respects them as a *Thou* rather than an *It*. Being physically present and emotionally available, the chaplain is in a place to experience something of the experience of the dying person and in so experiencing to allow the dying person to experience their own experience.

Comforting presence

The pervasive concern of chaplains is to bring 'spiritual comfort' to those for whom they care. As a *comforting presence*, chaplains offer comfort, not in an anodyne, 'tea and sympathy' sense, but in the original sense of the word 'to strengthen' (Latin: *confortare*). Chaplains aim to bring spiritual comfort through building relationships of trust, friendships where questions that are existentially urgent can be asked and can be given the kinds of honest, and occasionally unorthodox, replies that allow a dying person to find answers that are authentic and satisfying *to them*. Equally, chaplains bring spiritual comfort by their preparedness to remain with the authenticity of the other person's experience, often in a place beyond where words are effective.

Hopeful presence

Perhaps surprisingly, chaplains do not think specifically in terms of helping dying people find hope. Far from having specific interventions aimed at helping a person who is dying to navigate their way between hope (*sperare*) and despair (*desperare*), chaplains aim to model a way of being-*with* dying others that itself becomes a *hopeful presence*.

Chaplains reconceptualise hope as 'hope in the present' (CHP013.02) and, as such, are congruent with the traditional idea of being 'in a hopeful manner'. This agrees with what Marcel (2010) calls 'absolute' hope, which Garrard and Wrigley (2009) interpret as 'an overall stance towards life', which recognises the inevitable yet remains open to the possibility of experience and 'involves hope in others' (p.41). It also roots the achievement of being 'in a hopeful manner' in the importance of human relationship, a view that is supported by a number of hope researchers (Rumbold 1986; Herth 1990).

Conclusion

The emergence of this series of organic 'moments' between a chaplain and a dying person into what I am proposing as a theory of *chaplain as hopeful presence*, questions the perception that chaplains are primarily providers of religious care. This is the very narrow view of chaplains of those who argue that chaplaincy services have no place in a secular National Health Service and that the public purse should not be opened for such services.

Paley (2008a), for example, builds his philosophical objection to spiritual care as a concept appropriate to a secular health service on the basis that the UK is now a secular country. He argues, correctly, that there has been a sustained pattern of decline in UK Christianity and church attendance and, from this, he infers that spirituality (and, therefore, spiritual care) is of only minority interest (pp.177–8). Similarly, in a press release announcing a National Secular Society (NSS) report, 'Costing the heavens' (Christian 2011), Wood, Executive Director of the NSS, suggests that, while his organisation is not seeking to oust chaplains from hospitals:

their cost should not be borne by public funds, especially when clinical services for patients are being cut. We [the NSS] have proposed that chaplaincy services should be paid for through charitable trusts, supported by churches and their parishioners. If churches really support 'the big society' then they will stop siphoning off NHS cash to fund chaplains' salaries. (National Secular Society 2011)

Ironically, both Paley and the NSS are, at least to some extent, bolstered by the United Kingdom Board of Healthcare Chaplains (UKBHC) when it acknowledges that 'Board Registered Chaplains usually retain a distinctive religious identity because of the faith communities to which they are associated' (UKBHC). However, the Board goes on to enter the important caveat that:

because of their sensitivity, respect and understanding of other faith traditions and beliefs, Board Registered Chaplains are able to work across faith boundaries to explore spiritual and religious needs and to offer care and support. (UKBHC)

At issue is the fact that, while Paley and Wood differ in their misinterpretations of the facts, at root they are both united in fundamentally objecting to the involvement of religion in the public space. The difficulty is that they confuse religion and spirituality as the same species. However, the fact that 'spirituality' is presently such a contested concept in the healthcare literature (Paley 2008a, 2008b, 2008c, 2009a, 2009b, 2010; Leget 2008; Newsom 2008; Betts and Smith-Betts 2009; Hussey 2009; Nolan 2009b; Kevern 2010; see also Carrette and King 2005; Heelas and Woodhead 2005), and with it 'spiritual care' a disputed practice (Nolan 2011), is in large measure because for many people religion and spirituality are not the same thing. For better or worse, in the minds of many people, religion and spirituality have become uncoupled and, while it is the case that many healthcarers still confuse spiritual needs with religious needs, for many people the designation 'spiritual, but not religious' has real value (even if they struggle to articulate its meaning).

What is clear from this study is that the essential core of a chaplain's care, at least for those who work in a palliative setting, is care for the soul (Greek: *psyché*) of the dying other, which they do by the quality of their being-*with* the dying other. In many cases, this will involve supporting a person's religious practice, and chaplains do put proper emphasis on this kind of support. However, religious practice can be understood as *one* outward expression of an inward orientation, an expression of what Heelas and Woodhead (2005) term the sacralised 'subjective-life' (p.5). Non-religious people may express their inward orientation in non-religious ways; equally, they may not, or *they may not express it at all.*

The point is, as this study shows, that chaplains use skills developed in their spiritual formation – which for many, if not most (but not all), has been within a religious tradition – to attend to the inward orientation of a dying other: their sacralised 'subjective-life', their soul or *psyché*; in short, the inner being of those for whom they care. It is possible for a chaplain to deliver religious care without being present, in the sense of being-*with* a dying person. In contrast, spiritual care depends on a high degree of presence, such that I would conclude presence is *the* mode of spiritual care – certainly for people who are at the end of their life.

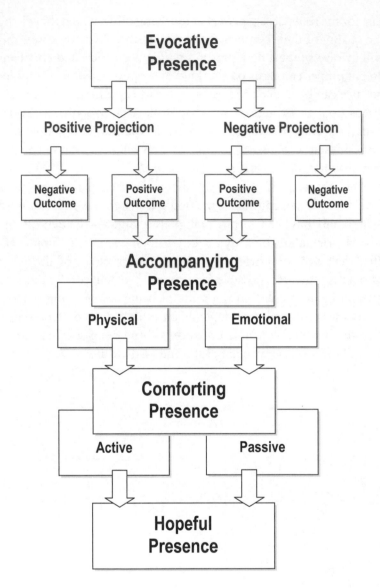

Figure 7.1 Chaplain as hopeful presence

Chapter 8

By Way of an Ending

A Personal View

Spiritual care, at least in a palliative setting, impacts the carer as much as it does the one cared for. It is no exaggeration to say that the work is transformative, life changing – I would suggest, life enhancing. To that degree, it might even be considered a form of spiritual practice. In what follows I try to describe the spiritual impact Chris had on me.

Some readers may feel that I overstepped the normal boundaries of professional conduct. This is because physical contact creates situations in which both carers and those for whom they care can be extremely vulnerable. An otherwise innocent touch may be misconstrued as a sexualised approach; an uninvited contact may be received as a form of physical assault. The regrettable fact is that some carers do deliberately exploit the power differential that is always implicit in a caring relationship and abuse those in their care in order to satisfy their own needs, whatever they may be.

It is understandable that professional carers would be cautious about touching – there is a great deal at stake: the well-being of the person being cared for; the carer's professional reputation. The issues are no less significant when set in the context of palliative care. However, the suggestion that a professional palliative carer should avoid physical contact with a dying person would be as ridiculous as it would be inhuman and lacking in compassion. The professional challenge is to recognise and respect the vulnerabilities of those with whom we work and to maintain the highest standards of personal and professional integrity in meeting them as fellow human beings and responding to their needs. This was my goal in working with Chris.

Chris: A birthday kiss

She was 84. At least that was the age announced by the two helium-filled balloons that buoyed each other, playfully, on the edge of the room. In fact, she was only 48! But the mischievous balloons were focus for a good laugh as we ate through some of the seven cakes bought and brought by friends, and commented sarcastically on the retro-playlist CD soundtrack, specially compiled for the day by an old school friend – including, among others, Stevie Wonder and The Osmonds: sounds from the 70s; music for dreamy-eyed, teenage girls to sing along to into their hairbrushes.

It was one of those muted celebrations: the room lined with 'thick-and-thin' friends, who had all shared in happier birthdays; banners draping themselves across the windows; cards standing on every bit of free shelf space; flowers, balloons; used cake plates and half-emptied cups and glasses ... and a hospital bed with its sleeping occupant, her morphine-limp hand held by her teenaged daughter.

Chris had been determined to make it to her birthday, and she had been able to experience something of the day. While I was in the room she 'rallied' and we swapped a few light-hearted words between us, then, when it was time for me to go, I lent forward and said, 'Let's have a birthday kiss then.'

The parting kiss had become a feature of my times with Chris. I'd got to know her over a couple of years during her intermittent, but increasingly protracted stays at the hospice. Normally, I don't do kissing, and to begin with, I didn't do kissing with Chris – although Chris did. She kissed and cuddled friends and nursing staff alike – but not me.

But then, on what was to become her penultimate admission, it happened – we kissed. It was one of those polite, 'air-kissy' things that makes a noise but avoids the risk of actual contact; barely cheek on cheek, and certainly no more. And so we started kissing, formally: when I arrived I greeted her with a holy, Pauline air-kiss and, when I got up to leave, we air-kissed our good-bye. Our kisses became the parentheses that marked the boundaries of our time together.

Somehow, kissing had become a thing Chris insisted upon. I was no longer 'allowed' in or out without pressing my cheek against hers.

And then it happened – again. Now bed bound, Chris had been wheeled through the door of her room so she could have her nicotine fix – three ciggies, one after the other; blue smoke hanging in a fug over her bed and trailing back into the room. It was not possible to get Chris fully outside, so lying in her bed she was half-in, half-out the door. I squeezed myself through the narrow gap between bed and doorpost.

'Have they told you – the nurses – have they told you?'

'No.' I did know Chris had had some news; but not what that news was.

'Maybe they'll tell you later.'

'Okay.'

'The doctor came in the night and told me I haven't got much longer to go. But that's okay. My friend's coming back to be with my daughter.'

I was holding Chris's hand. We had not had our ritual air-kiss and it felt appropriate now to lean in and be close. As I did there was something about this kiss that surprised me, something about it that felt different: I felt somehow more connected to Chris; there seemed somehow more intimacy between us than I'd known in the formalised kisses we had previously shared.

... There are two sorts of people lying in hospice beds: those who tell you about their world and those who ask about yours. Chris was in the second group. She did tell me about her world, but in a way that seemed to include me in it; she spoke about people as if I already knew them. But she also asked about my life, my wife, my kids, my weekend. And she was interested. So, being a good professional, I would tell her just enough to satisfy her interest and then return the focus to Chris and her situation.

This kiss, given now that she knew she was dying, connected me to Chris in a place beyond the chaplain-patient role-play that I always resist, but nonetheless get caught up in.

I had known that Chris valued my visits. Each time she was admitted she would ask for me and I always made a point of spending time with her to offer support. She'd known for a long time that she was seriously ill, but she was a strong, spirited woman; independent and determined. Twelve months previously a hospice doctor had told her that she probably wouldn't see Easter, but she 'unrealistically' focused on her 47th summer birthday and a year later she was equally decided about achieving her 48th – although now she was visibly fading. In the time I'd known her, Chris had spoken of her illness, but had never complained or appeared sorry for herself; she'd always been out-facing, forging firm relationships with others, a number of whom had subsequently died.

I lit her cigarette.

'There's things I need to sort out. I've got things on my mind.'

'Is that something you want to talk about?'

'Have you got time?'

'Yeah.'

'I keep thinking "Why me? What have I done to deserve this?" I'm only 48. It's too soon. When you look at all them others in the world … I've never done anything wrong. I've not been perfect, but I've never done anything bad.'

'It doesn't seem fair.'

'No!'

'I don't know why Chris.'

Later I met one of her visitors.

'It doesn't seem right. Why her?'

I wanted to say, 'Why not her? It's not her fault. That's just the way life goes sometimes.' But I shrugged and said, 'I don't know' …

Over the next few days, as we waited for her birthday, willing her towards her goal, I visited Chris regularly, sometimes meeting friends and family, sometimes by myself; each visit opened with our ritualised kiss, each visit closed with the same short ritual. Usually, I'd arrive in the middle of the day, after the nurses had attended to her, when Chris was clean and fresh. But one morning, anxious to know if she was still alive, I arrived before the nurses. Sitting next to her early morning body, I noticed strands of congealed mucus stretched like threads between her parted lips and smelled the stale odour that hung around her bed. Chris barely roused, and I don't know if she was aware that this visit did not begin or end as normal; without our kiss, it didn't feel like a real visit, but clearly I was facing the extent to which I felt able to be love incarnate.

Chris made it through her 48th birthday. She died in the early hours of the following morning. I wasn't told straightaway and only arrived after her family had left. The banners and balloons still hung in her room, but they were silent now, seemingly self-conscious about their misplaced well-wishing. I don't normally touch a dead body. I'm not squeamish; I've just never felt the need to. But I stroked Chris's face and bent to her forehead for one final good-bye kiss.

The people we meet touch our lives – some we always remember, some we can never forget; and some change us. Daniel changed me because he took me into a place I had never been before. He brought me *face à face* with the death anxiety I had managed happily to ignore, even though at that point I had been a hospice chaplain for some time. Daniel changed entirely the way I approach being-*with* a dying other; but he also opened the way for me to be changed in more subtle, more personal ways. Chris is among those who changed me in this spiritual sense.

From the beginning, our relationship was marked by the inevitability of its end. Chris was fun to be with. Even though she was clearly suffering, she enjoyed a laugh. She made friends of staff and others who were dying, exchanging 'phone numbers, keeping contact between visits, enquiring about people she had lost touch with and getting upset when they died. Like many who came within her circle, I had little option about becoming one of Chris's friends. To begin with, I kept a professional distance, holding my[real]self safely concealed behind the role of my[professional]self. But Chris quietly defied me to maintain this role-play, and over the weeks and months of her various admissions, I allowed her to melt my[real]self-protecting shield and I let my[real]self become more real with her.

Then Chris died. We knew she would and her death touched me; I felt her loss as an unfamiliar sadness. Some might accuse me of being 'unprofessional' and lacking 'boundaries'. But I was not and did not. Chris and I had laughed a lot together, but this was not inappropriate and I was always sensitive to my professional responsibilities towards her. As we walked together through the emotional landscape of her journey, where I was familiar with the terrain, I acted as her guide; and where, like Daniel, she led me into uncertain territory, I accompanied her and prayed with her. What I have come to appreciate, now that our journey has ended, is that being-*with* Chris, and others who are dying, has given me a unique opportunity for personal and spiritual growth; and that the sadness of loss is an important part of that growth. The nature of personal and spiritual growth is different in every person. For me, it has something to do with being more consciously aware that my living is impermanent and something to do with connecting consciously with the life of God as I encounter it, here and now, in those who touch my life. As Cooper (2010) puts it, it has something to do with trying to find a way to reply to the question, 'Can we suffer our aliveness?' (p.27).

Over the weeks spent preparing this book, I seem repeatedly to have been asked the same two questions. Simple and direct, the questions have come up in conversations with visitors, with people in hospice care and their relatives, with colleagues and with friends: 'How long have you been doing this job?' and 'Who do *you* talk to?'

The questions are not unreasonable, but I have begun to hear them as expressing the idea that working with dying people is in some way an heroic thing, a job that 'special' people do and perhaps for only a limited period. However, this perspective serves to romanticise palliative care and may actually be just another example of inauthentic everydayness, a means of insulating ourselves against the terrifying idea that *we ourselves will cease to be*. (I trust that I have not written anything that romanticises spiritual care with dying people, or over-inflated my involvement in it – there are no 'spiritual care experts'; each of us must begin afresh with every new person we meet.)

Yet, the two recurring questions also express compassion, a kindly concern for the well-*being* of the carer that raises the important question: who cares for the carers? The short answer, of course, is that professional healthcarers are all adults and as such, we should take responsibility for looking after ourselves. We need to know our limits and our triggers; we need to have good friends and outside interests; we need to eat well, take regular exercise, and get proper sleep. We need to be able to spot when we need a break and when we need to 'let-off-steam'; and where it is available, we especially need to make good use of supervision.

All of this is well-worn self-care advice for anyone who wants to sustain a career in healthcare (palliative or not). But I want to add to this the idea that the way we work with dying people can be its own resource for resilience. The experience of being-*with* people who are congruent with the fragility of their existence is rare and is itself a kind of gift from them (intentional or not) that can quicken growth in any of us who can be with them in the genuineness of our human *being*-ness. Such encounters are unique opportunities for enriching personal and spiritual growth, which can in the process transform our professional practice from the mere doing of something-*to* or -*for* the other into something that can enable both carer and cared-for to 'suffer our aliveness'. Chaplains may be the specialists who lead on spiritual care, but in my experience caring for the spirit of the other extends beyond chaplaincy: it is the essence of care and the core work of all healthcarers. Regarding healthcare in this way, as care for the human spirit, integrates the work of healthcarers, in all their diverse aspects, into a singular aspiration and translates healthcare practice from a functional occupation into what can be a fulfilling vocation. In my view, this modest shift in carer perspective has the potential to raise our healthcaring practice to the level of spiritual care and so have a profound impact on the well-*being* of ourselves and of those for whom we care.

Appendix

The Research Project

Introduction

In researching social relations, it is difficult to predict the directions a project is likely to take. I was clear from the start that the study would require a flexible (Robson 2002, pp.4–5) qualitative approach. I initially considered the Heuristic Inquiry Method, which Moustakas (1994) describes as a 'self-inquiry and dialogue with others aimed at finding the underlying meanings of important human experiences' (p.15). However, while Heuristic methodology is inherently spiritual (pp.11–14, *passim*), and while I was interested in chaplains' experience, I wanted to focus on processes, strategies and consequences (Flick 2002, p.50) of the experience, which implied the aim of (re)theorising practice.

As an alternative, Grounded Theory offers an abductive model of research and theory building, in which theory is developed from a systematic analysis of the data; the theory unfolding by constant comparison back to the data to ensure it remains grounded in the data. However, Grounded Theory largely retains the realist ontology that 'assumes an objective external reality' (Charmaz 2006, p.510); as such, epistemologically, it 'aims toward unbiased data collection, proposes a set of technical procedures, and espouses verification' (p.510). Fortunately, Grounded Theorists are debating the ontological/epistemological perspective of their method and Charmaz (2006) is among those foregrounding the pragmatic, Chicago School antecedents of the approach (p.183). She argues for 'an *interpretive rendering* of the worlds we study rather than an external reporting of events and statements' (p.184). For this reason, I decided to follow Charmaz's (2006) constructivist interpretation of Grounded Theory.

Research process
The project developed through three distinct phases:

Initial sampling (18 December 2008 – 23 February 2009)
For my initial sampling, I identified 22 chaplains working in 37 specialist palliative care units in London and southeast England (Ward 2008). I contacted six who were geographically accessible and identified four whose experience promised rich data and conducted a pilot interview. In all, I conducted five initial interviews.

Table A1 Base data –initial sampling

Code	Age	Gender	Religion	Lay / ordained	Experience (years)	
					Individual	Total
CHP001	40-50	Male	Anglican	Ordained	5	
CHP002	50-60	Male	Baptist	Ordained	6 (+3)*	
CHP003	50-60	Female	Anglican	Lay	7	
CHP004	60+	Male	Baptist	Ordained	10	
CHP005	50-60	Female	Anglican	Ordained	8	39 (+3)

* Some of the chaplains had additional experience in hospital chaplaincy.

The interviews followed an intensive style of unstructured interview aimed at 'eliciting each participant's interpretation of his or her experience' (Charmaz 2006, p.25). In each case, having explained my working definition of counselling[4] and having outlined Rumbold's (1986) model of hope development (see Chapter 1), I inquired how the chaplain worked with dying people and asked

---

4   The clinical environment in which palliative care chaplains work means that their interactions with those for whom they care are unpredictable and difficult to formalise; they are opportunistic and resist the traditional boundaries of the 50-minute counselling/therapy hour. For this reason, I used McLeod's (2003) definition of counselling that regards counselling as 'something that takes place when a person asks another person to listen, and help them to explore a problem in living, under conditions of confidentiality' (p.190).

them to relate any stories of their experiences with particular individuals. In essence, I was interested in three simple questions:

1. What was your experience?

2. How did you experience your experience?

3. How do you understand your experience?

The processes of initial and focused coding prompted an unexpected insight and I realised that, in formulating my question, I had *assumed* that palliative care chaplains are concerned to help dying people to find hope. Because this assumption was fundamental to my research question, I needed to check whether, and if so how, hope featured in the way palliative chaplains work with terminally-ill people.

In addition to problematising my assumptions, my coding of initial sampling data seemed to suggest an emergent theme concerned with how chaplains understand the way their *presence* as a religious person evokes positive and/or negative reactions (transferences) in those for whom they care, and how they, more or less consciously, work with what is evoked.

Chaplains' workshop (10 June 2009)

I had anticipated neither of these areas so, to explore them further, I conducted a chaplains' workshop at which I presented a summary of my findings to that point and posed two questions:

1. Should we as chaplains see ourselves as 'purveyors of hope'? (The term was borrowed from an interviewee [CHP004.09].)

2. In what ways (if at all) have a dying person's positive or negative reactions to you affected how you have offered them spiritual care?

The workshop was organised in association with the South East Region of the Association of Hospice and Palliative Care Chaplains (AHPCC) and hosted by a hospice within the region. Seventeen full-time, part-time and volunteer chaplains (plus the manager of a hospice Psychosocial and Spiritual Care Team) took part in the workshop. Sixteen interviewees were Christian, one was a female Muslim volunteer; three were among my five initial sampling interviewees.

Table A2 Base data – workshop

Code	Age	Gender	Religion	Lay / ordained	Experience (years)	
					Individual	Total
CHP011	50-60	Female	No Religion	Lay	–	
CHP012†	50-60	Female	Anglican	Lay	–	
CHP013†	60+	Male	Baptist	Ordained	–	
CHP014	50-60	Female	Muslim	Lay	0.1 (1 p/t)‡	
CHP015	60+	Female	Anglican	Ordained	–	
CHP016	60+	Female	Anglican	Ordained	–	
CHP017	60+	Female	Roman Catholic	Lay	10	
CHP018	60+	Male	Anglican	Religious Order	10 (+10)*	
CHP019	50-60	Female	Anglican	Ordained	0.3 (6 p/t)‡	
CHP020	50-60	Female	Anglican	Lay	0.25 (5 p/t)‡	
CHP021	40-50	Male	Anglican	Ordained	5	
CHP022	60+	Male	Anglican	Ordained	4.5	
CHP023	50-60	Female	Anglican	Lay	10	
CHP024	40-50	Female	Roman Catholic	Lay	4	
CHP025	60+	Male	Roman Catholic	Lay	0.2 (2 p/t)‡	
CHP026†	50-60	Male	Baptist	Ordained	–	
CHP027	50-60	Female	Baptist	Lay	6	
CHP028	50-60	Male	Anglican	Ordained	7	57.35 (+10)

Some of the chaplains had additional experience in hospital chaplaincy.
† Three chaplains were part of my initial sampling group.
*‡ Volunteer/part-time chaplain experience is regarded as 10 per cent full time
(i.e. 1 session per week).*

The workshop confirmed my understanding that the chaplains' evocative presence was an important emerging theme. But it also highlighted gaps in my knowledge that I felt demanded further clarification. In particular, the workshop highlighted something I had ignored in the initial interviews: the rather basic idea that chaplains provide *comfort*. While some of the initial interviewees had touched on the subject, my early negative attitude towards comfort (in the 'tea and comfort' sense) caused me to overlook its possible value in palliative care chaplains' care of dying people. I also realised I needed to understand more fully how a chaplain's presence evokes positive and/or negative reactions and how they work with what is evoked.

Theoretical sampling (16 July 2009 – 27 August 2009)

I returned to the field for three 'theoretical sampling' interviews (Charmaz 2006, p.100). To develop the conversation already begun, I decided to interview chaplains who had participated in the workshop and conducted three theoretical sampling interviews.

I had two specific interests I wanted to explore with my theoretical sample. I wanted more data about how chaplains' presence evokes positive and/or negative reactions and how chaplains work, more or less consciously, with what is evoked. I also wanted to understand how and in what ways chaplains provide comfort, which I had overlooked in my initial interviews. I began by asking my interviewees if they would 'take me into the intimacy of a meeting between you and a person you have cared for, and talk me through what might be a typical encounter.' I was interested to understand:

- how they approach a new relationship (expectations/fears/aims)

- how the relationship was shaped by their being a chaplain

- whether hope was an important theme in their work.

I also specifically enquired, 'What does it mean to comfort a dying person?'

In the event, my interviews with three chaplains gave me data that I considered saturated my theoretical categories. All interviewees were Christian, and one had been an initial sampling interviewee.

Table A3 Base data – theoretical sampling

Code	Age	Gender	Religion	Lay / ordained	Experience (years)	
					Individual	Total
CHP101	60+	Male	Anglican	Religious order	–	
CHP102	50-60	Female	Anglican	Ordained	–	
CHP103	60+	Male	Baptist	Ordained	–	–

* Some of the chaplains had additional experience in hospital chaplaincy.

Analytic method

Transcribing the interviews, I used the code-based theory building software package, N5™ (NUD•IST 5), to complete a combination of line by line and incident by incident initial coding for each transcribed interview. Using the 'constant comparative method' (Glaser and Strauss 1967, pp.105–113), I compared data with data to find similarities and differences and to make comparisons and contrasts (Charmaz 2006, p.54). Completing the first stage of initial coding and concept formation, I identified 61 tentative conceptual categories (Table A4).

The next stage of analysis focused coding and concept development, and I attempted to synthesise and begin explaining the larger segments of data (Charmaz 2006, p.57). To that end, I identified 'the most significant and/or frequent earlier codes', reducing the conceptual categories to nine analytic categories, finally identifying five theoretical categories as substantive codes that could 'relate to each other as hypotheses to be integrated into a theory' (p.63). In this, I was aiming to develop what Glaser and Strauss (1967) describe as substantive theory, 'developed for a substantive, or empirical, area of sociological inquiry, such as patient care' (p.32).

Table A4 Coding categories – conceptual; analytic; theoretical

Theoretical categories	Analytic categories	Conceptual categories
Not purveyors of hope	1. Sources of hope	1. Finding hope 2. Security is a source of hope 3. Losing hope 4. Helping people find hope
Being-*with*	2 Acting as chaplain	1. Wearing a (dog) collar 2. Chaplain's self-understanding of role 3. Chaplain's presence 4. Support/comfort 5. Impact on self 6. Fear/apprehension 7. Unwitting interventions 8. 'Creative discomfort' – countertransference 9. Care of self
	3. Religious interventions	1. Spiritual assessment 2. Bible reading (healing narrative) 3. Communion 4. Healing service 5. Funeral preparation 6. Discuss life after death 7. Prayer with person 8. 'Hold in heart' 9. Religious conversation 10. Challenge a person's ideas about God 11. Working with religious aspects
Evocative presence	4. Non-religious interventions	1. Hand holding 2. Being there 3. Opportunity to talk 4. Non-verbal communication: the gaze 5. Humour 6. Non-religious conversation

Table A4 Coding categories – conceptual; analytic; theoretical *cont.*

Theoretical categories	Analytic categories	Conceptual categories
Psycho-therapeutic categories	5. Psycho-therapeutic categories	1. UPR/Acceptance 2. Therapeutic relationship 3. Spiritual care as 'talking therapy' 4. Empathy: entering the other's despair 5. Active listening 6. Person-centred 7. Containing the gaze 8. Use of self 9. Transference
Miscellaneous	6. Metaphor	1. Journey 2. The dark place
	7. Existential issues	1. Non-existence 2. Isolation/separation
	8. Talk about dying	1. Stages of dying 2. Death anxiety (displacement)
	9. Miscella-neous	1. Human connection: establishing rapport 2. Palliate spirituality 3. Community 4. Face to the wall 5. Guilt 6. Referrals 7. Spiritual pain/spiritual need 8. Pilgrimage 9. Whose agenda? 10. Judgemental God 11. Working with/against religious projections 12. Frustration 13. Residual faith/reconnecting with faith 14. Helping people find peace 15. Multi-Disciplinary Team 16. Training

Credibility

McLeod (2003) lists nine criteria for evaluating qualitative data (pp.93–6) but, as Charmaz (2006) notes, 'Criteria for evaluating research depend on who forms them and what purposes he or she invokes' (p.182). An important criterion of evaluation is the degree to which the substantive theory is applicable to practice. Glaser and Strauss (1967) suggest four 'highly interrelated properties' (p.237) that should characterise Grounded Theory: it should 'closely *fit* the substantive area in which it will be used'; it should be 'readily *understandable*'; it should be 'sufficiently *general* to be applicable to ...daily situations within the substantive area'; and it should allow 'partial *control* over the structure and process of daily situations', by which they mean the theory should enable practitioners to read the situation and respond flexibly and appropriately as the situation develops (p.327).

To evaluate the credibility of my research I sent a summary to each one-to-one interviewee requesting they answer four questions:

1. How closely does the theory fit your experience?

2. Is the theory readily understandable?

3. Can the theory be generally applied to your daily work?

4. Would the theory help you read and respond flexibly to situations you encounter with those for whom they care?

Six of the seven responses were very positive.

Table A5 Credibility – participants' evaluation

	Fit	Understanding	Generality	Control
CHP001	The theory does fit my experience fairly well	...it made perfect sense	I think the theory can be applied to much of my daily work	...the theory could well help me to 'read and respond flexibly to situations'
*CHP002; CHP012	The theory fits my experience really well, there was very little there with which I couldn't identify	It is certainly clear and understandable (not only to Chaplains!)	It can generally be applied to my daily work and I found it very affirming	It would help me to respond flexibly and also to stand back and analyse what is often instinctive
*CHP003; CHP012	...it does feel very comfortable and fits in the situations that I have encountered and experienced	I believe so	The theory can be applied to our daily working practice	The theory does give flexibility
*CHP004; CHP013; CHP103	I resonated with a lot of what was being said	I think [this] will be an important piece of research	I find your model very helpful and, as you are aware, it follows much of what I believe to be the case anyway	...my only reservation is in the use of the phrase 'comforting presence' which can be misleading

Table A5 Credibility – participants' evaluation *cont.*

	Fit	Understanding	Generality	Control
CHP005	The overall theory does fit with my experience	...easy to understand	Yes	The transference element I think is deconstructed subconsciously and I will give the idea more thought in my practice. I will be more aware
*CHP018: CHP101	No reply	No reply	No reply	No reply
CHP102	I think this theory does fit my experience. I'm not sure I'd seen it that way before – had tried to structure it, but I think this is really good	Yes – I've not done any formal counselling or therapy training, but I could grasp what you were talking about	Yes – I might well try and reflect on some of my relationships with patients in the context of this framework	Yes – I hope it would

Some chaplains were interviewed more than once.

Ethical issues

Palliative care chaplains work closely with people who are dying and have a certain familiarity around death and dying. However, I was aware that I would be asking my participants to return, mentally and emotionally, into situations they may have found painful or distressing and which may be traumatic to recall. I had a duty of care towards my participants (McLeod 2003, pp.168–72) that required me to design safeguards into the project. Alongside ensuring that participation was voluntary and that confidentiality would be maintained (Madhavan 2007), I ensured participants had access to counselling/supervision (BACP 2009) should they need it and, on concluding the interview, I debriefed each participant and gave them a debriefing sheet.

For myself, it is worth noting that being-*with* the other 'in his death-bound solitude' is, as Levinas (1989) puts it, to answer the 'call to my responsibility' (p.125). This ethical response to the invocation that presages the bond with the other, which Levinas (1951) calls '*religion*', brings me into 'the relationship to a being as a being' (p.7), which is an encounter likely to foster spiritual growth. Notwithstanding this, I also had access to debriefing through my line manager and workplace supervisor, and if needed I could access my denominational counselling service.

The research was given ethical approval by the Research Ethics Committees of the Department of Psychology and Counselling, The University of Greenwich (5 November 2008), and Princess Alice Hospice (19 November 2008).

References

Ainsworth, M.D.S. (1991) 'Attachments and other Affectional Bonds across the Life Cycle.' In C.M. Parkes, J. Stevenson-Hinde and P. Marris (eds). *Attachment Across the Life Cycle*. London and New York: Routledge, pp.33–51.

Autton, N. (1968) *Pastoral Care in Hospitals*. Library of Pastoral Care. London: SPCK.

BACP (2009) *Ethical Framework for Good Practice in Counselling and Psychotherapy*. Lutterworth: British Association for Counselling and Psychotherapy.

Benzein, E. and Saveman, B.-I. (1998). 'One step towards the understanding of hope: A concept analysis.' *International Journal of Nursing Studies 35*, 322–329.

Betts, C.E. and Smith-Betts, A.F.J. (2009) 'Scientism and the medicalization of existential distress: A reply to John Paley.' *Nursing Philosophy 10*, 137–141.

Bowlby, J. (1998) *Attachment and Loss, Vol. 2. Separation: Anger and Anxiety*. London: Pimlico. (First published in 1973.)

Bowlby, J. (2005a) *The Making and Breaking of Affectional Bonds*. London and New York: Routledge. (First published 1979.)

Bowlby, J. (2005b) *A Secure Base: Clinical Applications of Attachment Theory*. London and New York: Routledge. (First published 1988.)

Brazier, D. (1995) *Zen Therapy*. London: Robinson.

Buber, M. (1958). *I and Thou*. (R.G. Smith, Trans.). Edinburgh: T & T Clark. (First published in German 1923.)

Buckley, J. and Herth, K. (2004) 'Fostering hope in terminally ill patients.' *Nursing Standard 19*, 10, 33–41.

Campbell, A.V. (1984) *Moderated Love: A Theology of Professional Care*. London: SPCK.

Camus, A. (2005) *The Myth of Sisyphus*. (J. O'Brien, Trans.). London: Penguin. (First published in French 1942.)

Carrette, J. and King, R. (2005) *Selling Spirituality: The Silent Takeover of Religion*. London and New York: Routledge.

Cassidy, S. (1988) *Sharing the Darkness: The Spirituality of Caring*. London: Darton, Longman and Todd.

Charmaz, K. (2006) *Constructing Grounded Theory: A Practical Guide Through Qualitative Analysis*. London: SAGE.

Chi, G.C-H-L. (2007) 'The role of hope in patients with cancer.' *Oncology Nursing Forum 34*, 2, 415–424.

Chochinov, H. (2007) 'Dignity and the essence of medicine: The A, B, C, and D of dignity conserving care.' *British Medical Journal 335*, 6 184–187.

Christian, R. (2011) 'Costing the heavens: Chaplaincy services in English NHS provider Trusts 2009/10.' London: National Secular Society.

Clarkson, P. (2003) *The Therapeutic Relationship* (2nd edn). London and Philadelphia: Whurr.

Cohen, R.A. (2006) 'Levinas: Thinking least about death – Contra Heidegger.' *International Journal for Philosophy of Religion 60*, 21–39.

Compact Oxford English Dictionary (2003) (2nd edn). Oxford and New York: Oxford University Press.

Cooper, M. and Adams, M. (2005) 'Death.' In E. van Deurzen and C. Arnold-Baker (eds) *Existential Perspectives on Human Issues: A Handbook for Therapeutic Practice.* Basingstoke: Palgrave Macmillan, pp.78–85.

Cooper, P. (2010) *The Zen Impulse and the Psychoanalytic Encounter.* New York and London: Routledge.

Cutcliffe, J.R. (2004) *The Inspiration of Hope in Bereavement Counselling.* London and Philadelphia: Jessica Kingsley Publishers.

Cutcliffe, J.R. and Herth, K. (2002) 'The concept of hope in nursing 1: Its origins, background and nature.' *British Journal of Nursing 11*, 12, 832–840.

Dass, R. (1971) *Be Here Now.* San Cristobal, New Mexico: Lama Foundation.

Dass, R. (1992) 'Death is not an outrage.' Ram Dass Tape Library. Retrieved 27 April 2011, from http://ramdasstapes.org/audiobook/dyi_081691.htm

de la Rochefoucauld, F. (2007) *Collected Maxims and Other Reflections.* (E.H. and A.M. Blackmore and F. Giguère, Trans.). Oxford: Oxford University Press. (First published in French in 1664.)

Dufault, K. and Martocchio, B.C. (1985) 'Symposium on compassionate care and the dying experience. Hope: its spheres and dimensions.' *Nursing Clinics of North America 20*, 2, 379–391.

Erikson, E.H. (1995) *Childhood and Society.* London: Vintage. (First published 1951.)

Erikson, E.H. (1997) *The Life Cycle Completed: Extended Version with New Chapters on the Ninth Stage of Development by Joan M. Erikson.* New York and London: W.W. Norton.

Farran, E.J., Herth, K.A. and Popovich, J.M. (1995) *Hope and Hopelessness: Critical Clinical Constructs.* Thousand Oaks, London, New Delhi: SAGE.

Felder, B.E. (2004) 'Hope and coping in patients with cancer diagnoses.' *Cancer Nursing, 27*, 4, 320–324.

Flick, U. (2002) *An Introduction to Qualitative Research* (2nd edn). London: SAGE.

Frankl, V. (2004) *Man's Search for Meaning.* (I. Lasch, Trans.). London: Rider. (First published in German 1946.)

Garrard, E. and Wrigley, A. (2009) 'Hope and terminal illness: False hope versus absolute hope.' *Clinical Ethics 4*, 38–43.

Glaser, B.G. and Strauss, A. (1967) *The Discovery of Grounded Theory: Strategies for Qualitative Research.* Chicago: Aldine de Gruyter.

Grof, C. and Grof, S. (1990) *The Stormy Search for the Self.* New York: Tarcher/Penguin.

Hanh, T.N. (1993) *The Blooming of a Lotus: Guided Meditation for Achieving the Miracle of Mindfulness.* (A. Laity, Trans.). Boston: Beacon Press.

Hanh, T.N. (2002) *No Death, No Fear: Comforting Wisdom for Life.* London: Rider.

Heard, D.H. and Lake, B. (1997) *The Challenge of Attachment for Caregiving.* London: Routledge.

Heelas, P. and Woodhead, L. (2005) *The Spiritual Revolution: Why Religion is Giving Way to Spirituality.* Oxford: Blackwell.

Heidegger, M. (1962) *Being and Time.* (J. Macquarrie and E. Robinson, Trans.). Oxford: Blackwell. (First published 1926.)

Heidegger, M. (1993) 'On the Essence of Truth.' In M. Heidegger, *Basic Writings* (J. Sallis, Trans.). London: Routledge, pp.111–138). (First published in English 1949.)

Herbert, R. (2006) *Living Hope: A Practical Theology of Hope for the Dying.* Peterborough: Epworth.

Herth, K. (1990) 'Fostering hope in terminally-ill people.' *Journal of Advanced Nursing 15*, 11, 1250–1259.

Herth, K. and Cutcliffe, J.R. (2002) 'The concept of hope in nursing 3: Hope and palliative care nursing.' *British Journal of Nursing 11*, 14, 977–983.

Hinksman, B. (1999) 'Transference and Countertransference in Pastoral Counselling.' In G. Lynch. (ed.) *Clinical Counselling in Pastoral Settings.* London and New York: Routledge, pp.94–106.

Hussey, T. (2009) 'Nursing and spirituality.' *Nursing Philosophy 10*, 71–80.

Jacobs, M. (1999) *Psychodynamic Counselling in Action* (2nd edn). London, Thousand Oaks, New Delhi: SAGE.

Johnson, S. (2007) 'Hope in terminal illness: An evolutionary concept analysis.' *International Journal of Palliative Nursing 13*, 9, 451–459.

Kavanaugh, K. (1989) 'Spanish Sixteenth Century: Carmel and Surrounding Movements.' In L. Dupré and D.E. Saliers (with J. Meyendorff) (eds) *Christian Spirituality Post-Reformation and Modern.* London: SCM Press, pp.69–92.

Kevern, P. (2010) 'Can reductionists be chaplains too? Reflections on the vacuousness of "spirituality".' *Scottish Journal of Healthcare Chaplaincy 13*, 2, 2–8.

Kübler-Ross, E. (1969) *On Death and Dying.* London: Macmillan.

Ladkin, D. (2006) 'When deontology and utilitarianism aren't enough: how Heidegger's notion of "dwelling" might help organisational leaders resolve ethical issues.' *Journal of Business Ethics, 65*, 87–98.

Laplanche, J. and Pontalis, J-B. (1973) 'Phantasy (or Fantasy).' In J. Laplanche and J-B. Pontalis (eds) *The Language of Psychoanalysis* (D. Nicholson-Smith, Trans.). London: Karnac Books, pp.314–319.

Leget, C. (2008) 'Spirituality and nursing: why be reductionist? A response to John Paley.' *Nursing Philosophy 9*, 277–278.

Levinas, E. (1951) 'Is Ontology Fundamental?' In E. Levinas (2006) *Entre Nous: Thinking of the Other* (M.B. Smith and B. Harshav, Trans.). London and New York: Continuum, pp.1–10.

Levinas, E. (1957) 'Lévy-Bruhl and Contemporary Philosophy.' In E. Levinas (2006) *Entre Nous: Thinking of the Other.* (M.B. Smith and B. Harshav, Trans.). London and New York: Continuum, pp.34–45.

Levinas, E. (1969) *Totality and Infinity.* (R.A. Cohen, Trans.). Pittsburg: Dequene University Press.

Levinas, E. (1989) 'From the One to the Other: Transcendence and Time.' In E. Levinas (2006) *Entre Nous: Thinking of the Other* (M.B. Smith and B. Harshav, Trans.). London and New York: Continuum, pp.114–132.

Levinas, E. (1999) *Alterity and Transcendence.* (M. B. Smith, Trans.). New York: Columbia University Press.

Levine, R. (2007) 'Treating idealized hope and hopelessness.' *International Journal of Group Psychotherapy 57*, 3, 297–317.

Levine, S. (1986) *Who Dies? An Investigation of Conscious Living and Conscious Dying.* Dublin: Gateway.

Lines, D. (2006) *Spirituality in Counselling and Psychotherapy.* London: SAGE.

MacLeod, R. and Carter, H. (1999) 'Health professionals' perception of hope: Understanding its significance in the care of people who are dying.' *Mortality 4*, 3, 309–317.

McLeod, J. (2003) *Doing Counselling Research* (2nd edn). London: SAGE.

McCluskey, U. (2005) *To Be Met as a Person: The Dynamics of Attachment in Professional Encounters.* London and New York: Karnac.

McSherry, W. (2001) 'Spiritual Crisis? Call a Nurse.' In H. Orchard (ed.) *Spirituality in Health Care Contexts.* London: Jessica Kingsley, pp.107–117.

McSherry, W. (2006) *Making Sense of Spirituality in Nursing and Health Care Practice: An Interactive Approach* (2nd edn). London: Jessica Kingsley Publishers.

McSherry, W. and Jamieson, S. (2011) 'An online survey of nurses' perceptions of spirituality and spiritual care.' *Journal of Clinical Nursing 20*, 1757–1767.

Madhavan, M. (2007) Data Protection Overview. Retrieved 27 April 2011, from www.jisclegal.ac.uk/Portals/12/Documents/PDFs/dataprotection.pdf

Marcel, G. (2010) *Homo Viator: Introduction to the Metaphysic of Hope.* (E. Craufurd and P. Seaton, Trans.). South Bend, Indiana: St Augustine's Press. (First published in French 1945.)

Matthews, E. (1996) *Twentieth-Century French Philosophy.* Oxford and New York: Oxford University Press.

Moltmann, J. (1967) *Theology of Hope.* (J.W. Leitch, Trans.). London: SCM Press. (First published in German 1965.)

Monroe, B. and Oliviere, D. (eds) (2007) *Resilience in Palliative Care: Achievement in Adversity.* Oxford: Oxford University Press.

Moustakas, C. (1994) *Phenomenological Research Methods.* Thousand Oaks, CA: SAGE.

National Secular Society (2011) 'Study shows that spending on hospital chaplains provides no clinical benefit.' Retrieved 27 April 2011, from www.secularism.org.uk/study-shows-that-spending-on-hos.html

Nekolaichuk, C.L. and Bruera, E. (1998) 'On the nature of hope in palliative care.' *Journal of Palliative Care 14*, 1, 36–42.

Nekolaichuk, C.L., Jevne, R.F. and Maguire, T.O. (1999) 'Structuring the meaning of hope in health and illness.' *Social Science and Medicine 48*, 591–605.

Newsom, R.W. (2008) 'Comments on "Spirituality and nursing: a reductionist approach" by John Paley.' *Nursing Philosophy 9*, 214–217.

Nolan, S. (2008a) 'Am I a male social worker?' *PlainViews 5*, 6. Retrieved 27 April 2011, from http://plainviews.healthcarechaplaincy.org/archive/AR/c/v5n6/pp.html

Nolan, S. (2008b) '"The experiencing of experience": A Pragmatic reassessment of Rogerian phenomenology.' *European Journal of Counselling and Psychotherapy 10*, 4, 323–339.

Nolan, S. (2009a) 'Hope.' In M. Watson, C. Lucas, A. Hoy and J. Wells (eds) *The Oxford Handbook of Palliative Care* (2nd edn). Oxford: Oxford University Press, pp.xxix–xxxiii.

Nolan, S. (2009b) 'In defence of the indefensible: An alternative to John Paley's reductionist, atheistic, psychological alternative to spirituality.' *Nursing Philosophy 10*, 203–213.

Nolan, S. (2011) 'Psychospiritual care: New content for old concepts – towards a new paradigm for non-religious spiritual care.' *Journal for the Study of Spirituality 1*, 1, 50–64.

Paley, J. (1996) 'How not to clarify concepts in nursing.' *Journal of Advanced Nursing 24*, 572–578.

Paley, J. (2008a) 'Spirituality and secularization: Nursing and the sociology of religion.' *Journal of Clinical Nursing 17*, 175–186.

Paley, J. (2008b) 'Spirituality and nursing: A reductionist approach'. *Nursing Philosophy 9*, 3–18.

Paley, J. (2008c) 'The concept of spirituality in palliative care: An alternative view'. *International Journal of Palliative Nursing 14*, 9 448–452.

Paley, J. (2009a) 'Religion and the secularisation of health care.' *Journal of Clinical Nursing 18*, 1963–1974.

Paley, J. (2009b) 'Doing justice to the complexities of spirituality and religion in a pluralistic world.' *Journal of Clinical Nursing 18*, 3512–3513.

Paley, J. (2010) 'Spirituality and reductionism: three replies.' *Nursing Philosophy 11*, 178–190.

Pruyser, P. (1963) 'The phenomenology and dynamics of hoping.' *Journal for the Scientific Study of Religion 3*, 1, 86–96.

Reynolds, M.A.H. (2008) 'Hope in adults, ages 20–59, with advanced stage cancer.' *Palliative and Supportive Care 6*, 259–264.

Risjord, M. (2009) 'Rethinking concept analysis.' *Journal of Advanced Nursing 65*, 3, 684–691.

Robson, C. (2002) *Real World Research: A Resource for Social Scientists and Practitioner-researchers* (2nd edn). Oxford: Blackwell.

Rodgers, B.L. (2000) 'Philosophical Foundations of Concept Development.' In B.L. Rodgers and K.A. Knafl (eds) *Concept Development in Nursing: Foundations, Techniques and Applications.* Philadelphia: W.B. Saunders Company, pp.7–38.

Rogers, C.R. (1980) *A Way of Being.* Boston: Houghton Mifflin.

Rogers, C.R. (2004) *On Becoming a Person: A Therapist's View of Psychotherapy.* London: Constable. (First published 1961.)

Rousseau, P. (2000) 'Hope in the terminally ill'. *Western Journal of Medicine 173*, 117–118.

Rumbold, B.D. (1986) *Helplessness and Hope: Pastoral Care in Terminal Illness.* London: SCM Press.

Saunders, C. (1988) 'Spiritual pain'. *Journal of Palliative Care 4*, 3, 29–32.

Saunders, C. (1996) 'Foreword.' In M. Kearney (ed.) *Mortally Wounded: Stories of Soul Pain, Death and Healing.* Dublin: Marino Books, pp.11–12.

Saunders, C. (2005) 'Foreword.' In D. Doyle, G. Hanks, N.I. Cherny, K. Calman (eds) *Oxford Textbook of Palliative Medicine* (3rd edn). Oxford: Oxford University Press, pp.xvii–xx.

Smith-Stoner, M. and Frost, L. (1998) 'How to build your "hope skills".' *Nursing 29*, 9, 48–51.

Stern, D.N. (1985) *The Interpersonal World of the Infant: A View from Psychoanalysis and Developmental Psychology*. New York: Basic Books.

Swift, C. (2009) *Hospital Chaplaincy in the Twenty-First Century: The Crisis of Spiritual Care on the NHS*. Farnham, Surrey and Burlington, VT: Ashgate.

United Kingdom Board of Healthcare Chaplains (*n.d.*). 'Faith and belief communities.' Retrieved 27 April 2011, from www.ukbhc.org.uk/employers/faith-and-belief-communities

Wade, P. (2010) 'The psychological impact of living with cancer.' *Myeloma Matters* (Spring), 17–20.

Walter, T. (1997) 'The ideology and organization of spiritual care: Three approaches.' *Palliative Medicine 11*, 1, 21–30.

Ward, D. (2008) *Hospice and Palliative Care Directory: United Kingdom and Ireland*. London: Hospice Information.

Watson, M., Lucas, C., Hoy, A. and Wells, J. (eds) (2009) *The Oxford Handbook of Palliative Care* (2nd edn). Oxford: Oxford University Press, pp.xxix–xxxiii.

Watts, F., Nye, R. and Savage, S. (2002) *Psychology for Christian Ministry*. London and New York: Routledge.

Weisman, A. (1972) *On Dying and Denying: A Psychiatric Study of Terminality*. New York: Behavioural Publications.

West, W. (2004) *Spiritual Issues in Therapy: Relating Experience to Practice*. Basingstoke and New York: Palgrave Macmillan.

Winnicott, D.W. (1954a) 'Metapsychological and Clinical Aspects of Regression within the Psycho-analytical Set-up.' In D.W. Winnicot (1984) *Through Paediatrics to Psychoanalysis: Collected Papers*. London: Karnac, pp.278–294.

Winnicott, D.W. (1954b) 'Withdrawal and Regression.' In D.W. Winnicot (1984) *Through Paediatrics to Psychoanalysis: Collected Papers*. London: Karnac, pp.255–261.

Yalom, I.D. (1980) *Existential Psychotherapy*. New York: Basic Books.

Yalom, I. D. (2000) Religion and psychiatry. Retrieved 27 April 2011, from http://web.comhem.se/u68426711/14/Yalom00.pdf

Yalom, I.D. (2008) *Staring at the Sun: Overcoming the Dread of Death*. London: Piatkus.

Subject Index

Author Index